Change Reaction

Securing a Positive Reaction to Change

OTIS JOHNSON

ISBN 978-1-64140-319-1 (paperback)
ISBN 978-1-64140-320-7 (digital)

Christian Faith Publishing, Inc.
832 Park Avenue
Meadville, PA 16335
www.christianfaithpublishing.com

Printed in the United States of America

Table of Contents

The study, on which this book is based, contributes to positive corporate and social change by providing leadership with information in guiding creation of a supportive work environment during organizational change and to inspire employees to contribute to business innovation, while creating skilled jobs and generating profit. Corporations generally have objectives related to corporate social responsibility, but the supporting projects are usually focused on philanthropy or environmental-friendly practices. This chapter presents ways to partially achieve these types of objectives by virtue of the way change is handled within the organization.

Employees respond to change, such as mergers and acquisitions, either by supporting or resisting it. With a grounding in the understanding of the pain points from an employee perspective, managers will have a clearer emotional intelligence from an employee perspective, which will enable them to be better managers.

A key driver of the significance of this book is the potential to avoid one of the common negative outcomes of change: the costly consequence of losing talented employees (or worse, keeping them at half the focus required to succeed). The annual cost of employee turnover at a company with 1,000 employees is over two million dollars. Change initiatives have not traditionally focused on people as the primary target. In part two we look at this and why that trend needs to change.

Knowledge of these predictors is crucial for developing effective change management strategies that minimize the potentially disruptive effects on employees and business operations. The Author addresses the lack of knowledge and understanding about employee response to change by examining whether any of four factors (initial change reaction, change communication, involvement in change development, and perceived change success) predict employee response to large-scale change initiatives.

Recent studies have shown that the manner and the degree to which employees are included in change implementation, enhances their organization's successful transition to a new working reality. While change leaders of an organization may have a clear vision of the planned change, they might not have considered whether the organization was ready for change at its most essential level, the employee base. Change communication refers to the manner in which management conveys information relevant to the proposed change to employees, as well as the frequency.

The two primary dependent variables in this research were reaction to change (RC), which includes the full spectrum of reactions ranging from active resistance to championing change and support of change (SC), which is further explored in three separate measures: compliance with change (CM), cooperation with change (CP), and championing of change (CH).

Large-scale change initiatives, if executed well, can reinforce an employee's commitment to their work and organization. The Author approaches employee involvement in change as a multidimensional construct, which at its core focuses on the emotional dimensions of employee commitment to change.

Employees may have an interest in organizational change not only as employees (how the change will affect their day-to-day operations) but also as stakeholders (the overall effect of change on the organization's success and well-being). Perceived change success refers to the degree to which employees perceived the proposed change to be completely and effectively implemented.

Change of the magnitude of an organizational restructure, whether due to mergers and acquisitions or other drivers, has the potential to disrupt a company's performance, success, and growth if not handled effectively and efficiently.

A huge factor in predicting reaction and the subsequent success of a change implementation is for employees at all levels to understand not only the 'new model' but to understand what happens to the old model. Here we look at the way change is introduced by identifying what is going to stay the same, what is going away and what is going to be new and why it should be better for each level of employee in the organization.

No matter how generous the benefits and accommodating the workplace environment, if employees have bad relationships with their managers, they are likely to give up the perks of a position for one that may have fewer benefits, but a better manager.

Because of its ubiquity and inevitability, large-scale change represents potential organizational discontinuity and, consequently, effective change management has become a major component of organizational success. The Author wraps up with a practical guide and examples to implementing the 4 key predictors of a successful outcome.

Part 1

The Only Constant Is Change

1 The Problem - Why Stasis and Business Don't Mix

In business and in life, we often hear about how much people hate change. This generalization is in direct opposition to the axiom that the only constant is change. Like opposing political parties, these two camps are here to stay, and the sooner we learn to manage them, the sooner we can stop being conflicted by them and become successful in our efforts to create effective and positive change.

The fact is that people do not really hate change. We go on vacations, move homes, buy new things, look for a change of pace, and celebrate these moments. What we hate is not having a say in the change. I didn't start my career seeking to be a change management expert. I became one as a result of constant change happening in all of the places I worked. In hindsight, going into the pharmaceutical industry, I probably should have known that change was going to be the norm in my working life. I was about six years into my job in the clinical research area—where I co-authored protocols for clinical trials of new and marketed drugs—when my eye for efficiency segued from my writing of protocols and clinical study reports, to actually managing and improving various aspects of the clinical trial processes themselves. It wasn't so much a planned career track, as it was doing what needed to be done to improve the way we worked. I've always been one of those guys who jumps in regardless of whether it is in my job

9

description or not and, in this case, it's where my degree in business management came in handy. So, when Management announced that there was going to be a foundational redesign in the structure of science and operations, I was all on board before even hearing the details. I was a proponent of change that was geared toward an efficient workflow. I had been managing change within my team for quite some time and now thought the powers that be were boarding my ship.

Imagine my surprise when I was told that only employees with the word *manager* in their job title would be able to have a leadership role in managing this foundational change. I was hurt, angry, offended, and afraid all at once. Here I had been initiating and managing the efficiency of our clinical trial processes for years, with no regard to the wording of my job title, and now I was going to be left out of the process of solidifying significant scientific and operational change. Once I bandaged my offended ego, I talked with my department head, and the job title limitation was removed from the manager selection process, and I was given one of the roles in the new structure. As the natural order would have it, I was asked to participate in leading a key component of the new initiative, which was intended to improve the efficiency of the scientific and clinical operations divisions at the company. This project led to a positive change in the execution of clinical trials.

Initially, we were focused on better country and site selection, and improved predictability through patient recruitment planning. This later changed to include a rigorous analytics process that enabled us to show that our team's projects were more likely to finish on time. These performance metrics were largely responsible for our full team making it through a large merger fully intact, while there were large employee reductions in other parts of the company. This was just the start of me helping organizations manage large-scale change by looking at it from a different, data-driven perspective. Now, many years later, I am able to share that perspective with you, along with some primary research findings, to help improve your chances of having a successful change initiative.

The pharmaceutical industry has almost always been synonymous with mergers, but in recent years many business sectors have seen a major change, through either mergers and acquisitions or internal restructures. Even if the change is not driven by corporate valuation, with the rapid pace of technological advancements, every type of business has to change in order to keep up and stay competitive.

According to The Institute for Mergers and Acquisitions Alliances, in 2015, companies announced over 44,000 transactions with a total value of more than 4.5 trillion USD. There are no all-inclusive statistics for the number and financial implications of internal organizational change, done as a part of daily business practices and have nothing to do with mergers and acquisitions. Chances are, however, is that if you've picked up this book, you are keenly aware that these smaller changes within an organization are far more common than the ones that make Wall Street headlines. One new-hire in the executive offices of a company can call for change that has far-reaching implications on the business as a whole. New chief executives often feel compelled to reorganize their companies, and in many cases, this is why they were hired. In fact, nearly half of newly hired CEO's launch some kind of reorganization during their first two years on the job. Even the hiring of a new principal at a public school, or a new manager of a local business, is never done without affecting every employee, and everyone who interacts with the establishment. These hires may be inevitable or sorely needed, and even though people are surrounded by change on a regular basis, the reaction to it is rarely the same or predictable.

Corporate reorganizations are risky investments of time, energy, and resources, and many do little to improve the business. Chrysler restructured its organization three times in the three years preceding its bankruptcy, and eventually combined with Fiat to little or no effect. A recent Bain & Company study of fifty-seven major reorganizations found that less than one-third produced any meaningful improvement in performance. Some actually destroyed value.[1]

Whether you are promoting from within or merging companies, change at any level is costly and often risky. The expensive and high-risk nature of large-scale organizational change has the potential to disrupt not only company productivity and revenue but also employee commitment at a crucial time. Some analysts claim that

---

[1] Forbes.com: http://onforb.es/22DZ86Q

for change to be successful it should minimize disruption, when in reality the whole idea of change is to be disruptive—if we are in a position of stasis, we are not really changing and we certainly aren't growing. If we are not still and not growing, the only other option is to be changing negatively toward death. So the key is not to minimize disruption but to manage and plan for disruption so that it results in a positive and successful outcome where we end up in a better place.

This analysis begs the question, why do so many employees balk when management announces plans of organizational change intended to make the company strong and poised for growth with new and improved processes, tools, technology, services, and products? Because to tout something as new and improved infers that the current model— the one they've been staking their careers on—is old and broken. It is like gifting a makeover for your loved one on their birthday. No matter how much it needs to happen, it still hurts to face the fact that something so personal to you is broken—especially when the bomb is dropped without a clue as to the motive behind this new and improved model.

Because of its ubiquity and inevitability, large-scale change represents potential organizational discontinuity and, consequently, effective change management has become a major component of organizational success. The fact that corporate change has become commonplace in the global economy has led many to seek to under-stand change management. But in seeking to understand, few have looked at change management from the perspective of employees who are the target of change, or have analyzed what factors predict or influence how these employees may react to the news of change— reactions that will help lead to the successful implementation of it. As a result, 50–80 percent of mergers and acquisitions fail because of clashing corporate cultures, a lack of clear communication, and a lack of employee involvement in the change.

While nearly all organizational change is decided at the top or executive level, it usually needs to be implemented from the ground up and involve employees at the lowest levels of the organizational hierarchy. However, this apparent disconnect in efforts to under-stand change management is not the obvious, executive-to-employee dynamic. It is often the most nuanced difference between the terms *leadership* and *management*.

Generally speaking, leadership is when a person influences a group to achieve a common goal, and management is a collaboration of the allocation of people and resources to accomplish the goal. This may sound like semantics but as my experience illustrates, management is a team sport and leadership is its coach. Without the team, nobody wins. Picture a totem pole; the low man has to hold everyone else up, even the man at the very top.

Change leaders put in place to drive initiatives and inspire staff toward big picture implementation might overlook such details as the resource requirements and monitoring needed during change implementation that a change manager is put in charge of. Yet, a change manager might not have the skillset required to inspire and shepherd change for the sake of the bigger picture. Change leaders of an organization may have a clear vision of what to change, but they may not have considered whether the organization was ready for change, and often do not consider how they might measure successful change afterward.[2]

For those senior executive stakeholders, one of the common, negative outcomes of change is the costly consequence of losing talented employees—or worse, keeping them at half the focus required for success. Turnover is costlier for higher complexity jobs,[3] such as those in the pharmaceutical industry, than it is for lower complexity ones. Even so, the estimated cost of employee turnover, averaged for all business sectors, is close to $14,000 per employee, with the annual cost of employee turnover at a company with 1,000 employees at over two million dollars.[4] Regardless of where you are on the totem

---

[2] Whelan-Berry, K., and Somerville, K. (2010). Linking change drivers and the organizational change process: A review and synthesis. Journal of Change Management, 10(2), 175–193. doi:10.1080/14697011003795651

[3] Hinkin, T., & Tracey, J. (2010). What makes them so great? An analysis of human resources practices among Fortune's best companies to work for. Cornell Hospitality Quarterly, 51(2), 158–170.

[4] Based on data from the Bureau of Labor Statistics, O'Connell, M., & Kung, M. (2007). The cost of employee turnover. Industrial Management, 49(1), 14–19. http://industrialmanagement.epubxp.com

pole, wouldn't it be nice to save your company this amount of money *and* implement change to stay competitive in your career?

Having worked for larger pharmaceutical companies, ranging from 10,000 to 100,000 individuals, my analytical mind had a field day exploring ways to approach change implementation. And despite the brief blow to my ego—once details emerged in one of my earlier experiences with large-scale change—my reaction rapidly changed to that of a champion of change. Once the issue was cleared up, I was excited and engaged.

In addition to change that is geared toward maintaining a competitive stance in the marketplace, corporations generally have objectives related to corporate social responsibility, but these initiatives are usually focused on philanthropy or environmental-friendly practices. However, by understanding what drives the reaction to change, it is possible to achieve these social responsibility objectives by virtue of a new and improved operational change within the organization. For instance, pharmaceutical companies have a responsibility to shareholders to provide them with value in the form of a strong return on their investment; but the nature of pharmaceutical products (medicines, medical devices, vaccines), creates a compelling need for ethical consideration and treatment of other stakeholders, such as patients, the environment, and employees. Seeing beyond the profit motive in this example can be challenging, but implementing processes that strike a balance between social value and financial value can only improve employee loyalty, which in turn creates a willingness to be open to contributing to a process that supports a better end state.

As a clinical research professional, I have been fortunate to be part of an industry whose success can lead to great social change, because our efforts are geared toward creating medicines that meet health needs and improve the quality of life of individuals around the world. This certainly helps employees, at all levels, feel good about their choice of career, but given the size and competitive nature of the industry, persistent change can still be overwhelming, regardless of the company's social good.

Why change what isn't broken? Depending on the company, many individual contributors and employees lower down the organizational hierarchy won't understand the need for a change that requires high-level meetings, training on implementation, and a disruption to their everyday work environment. It is fair to say that, in the majority of instances, executive management has started implementing change long before it is announced to the general staff who may be so cocooned in their daily role that they can't see the big picture. Although these high-level decisions and early implementation processes are understandable, the employees who will have to implement the change, are more likely to have a positive reaction if they are included sooner rather than later. Don't underestimate the power of initial change reaction. The truth remains: there is only one chance to make a first impression.

By now, it is clear that change is the only constant in our working lives, so let's add one more ingredient to the cumbersome and often emotional mix. Based on recent research, the change management history of an organization, and its employees' previous experiences of organizational change, affect future change management and implementation. In addition to having her hands full, a new CEO has to worry about her predecessor. If her predecessors tried to institute change with less than stellar results, the new leader is at a disadvantage from day one. Change management research has, for the most part, overlooked the role of an organization's change management history in shaping employee attitudes when introducing new changes.[5] Employees who experienced poor change management in the past are inclined to react poorly when any more change implementation plans are announced. More specifically, previous poor experiences led to decreased openness to change, job satisfaction, and trust, as well as increased cynicism and turnover intentions. This reality brings up the most devastating of all "change" mantras: *the more things change the more they stay the same,"*—the death knell to a business trying to adjust and stay competitive.

---

[5] Bordia, Restubog, Jimmieson, and Irmer (2011)

Many companies approach change through what is called business process reengineering (BPR), a strategic tool for managing transformational organizational change intended to improve an organization's performance. BPR is "the fundamental rethinking and redesign of business processes to achieve dramatic improvements in critical, contemporary measures of performance, such as cost, quality, service, and speed."[6] While some high-profile corporations such as Taco Bell, Kodak, IBM Credit Corporation, and Hallmark, are used as case studies of successfully employed BPR to improve their existing business conditions and maintain a competitive advantage, many more fail. One of the biggest factors that led to these failures was that there was no success in gaining dedicated, long-term commitment from management and the employees. Bringing people on board is a difficult task and many BPR change initiatives never take off because not enough effort is put into securing support. One of the most obvious adverse effects of a company's decision to re-engineer is lowered employee morale. Most people are wary of change and are not able to adapt to it easily. But remember, people don't dislike change, they dislike not having a say in it.

So far, we have three categories of change all of which result in personnel upheavals:

- Financially driven organizational change that often involves mergers and acquisitions;
- Internal organizational change, often driven by implementing new technologies; and
- Managerial change of new-hires at the executive level that trickle down to organizational change.

Each of these could be fighting an unaccounted-for, uphill battle if previous changes within the organization were not successful. Are we still contemplating whether people hate change?

---

[6] Goksoy, A., Ozsoy, B., & Vayvay, O. (2012). Business process reengineering: Strategic tool for managing organizational change an application in a multinational company. International Journal of Business and Management, 7(2), 89–112. doi:10.5539/ijbm.v7n2p89

Let's not forget the added variable of social standing. As described with my example of the pharmaceutical industry's far-reaching impact, employees may have an interest in organizational change not only as employees (how the change will affect their day-to-day operations), but also as social stakeholders (the overall effect of change on the organization's success and well-being, and how that relates to society as a whole). Businesses today have to answer calls for social change. Be they environmentally-inspired, sustainability issues or broader socio-economic issues, today's consumers often drive business operations and its need for change.

Sustainable organizational change requires a balanced approach that acknowledges stakeholder needs. Change that focuses exclusively on the traditional bottom line of reducing production cycle time, and operating costs—while increasing productivity and revenue for the business at the expense of stakeholder concerns and social responsibility—probably won't facilitate an organization's sustainable future.[7] While all of these factors may be conceptualized at first by the financial benefits of change, these benefits may never be realized if the implementation does not take into consideration that all changes have an emotional component that is directly related to employee engagement with—and commitment to—organizational change.

Given the substantial opportunity for social change in my profession, coupled with the sector's ubiquitous change—many driven by mergers and acquisitions—it is important to create an environment in which employees have the best opportunity to be successful for themselves, their team and their organization. Now, I am happy to share some data and insights to help you create such a work environment. Regardless of the size and nature of your business, change is constant. Change is life. *How* a business goes about making changes is just as important as the changes themselves.

---

[7] Garvare, R., & Johansson, P. (2010). Management for sustainability – A stakeholder theory. Total Quality Management & Business Excellence, 21(7), 737–744. doi:10.1080/14783363.2010.483095

2 Personal vs. Professional Life

People tend to treat repetitive responsibilities and habitual behavior as a source of comfort. If we all knew what was going to happen at every given moment for the rest of our working lives, we would build our personal lives accordingly, and never be fearful that our bosses may come down on us, the company that we work for will be bought out, or that our jobs (and paychecks) may disappear. We would know exactly how much we will earn over the course of our lives and, consequently, how much we should and could save, and how much importance to put on individual tasks and daily commutes. As boring as that may sound to some, to others, it may bring an extreme sense of relief and security. There's another group who, based on this knowledge, know that their time with the company is numbered. In the next year or two, they will move on to something else. Do you want to bet on how much effort they will put into their daily tasks until then? How well employees perform their job depends on many things, many of which are out of their employer's control. However, an employer can influence their performance by executing change well, using some of the insights from this book.

When we've become so comfortable with a process that it comes naturally, we refer to it as being in a groove. Of course, when that groove feeds a company's bottom line, the powers that be may equate a staff member's comfortable groove to a rut—one that the whole company needs to get out of. There is a legitimate argument that being in a comfortable groove may very well be a sign that it is time for a change.

Employees who love their job, and feel good about the company they work for, may well be among the ones most resistant to a change. After all, they are content, maybe even avid cheerleaders of the day-to-day activities. They have hit their stride and are feeling groovy. So, when a corporate leader, who they only see at company-sponsored events, comes along and says, "We are going to shift gears," it may be enough to send them into an emotional tailspin. Whereas, someone who seems to be plodding along on the daily task track may feel that change is long overdue, and that it is time to get out of their rut and jump on board as soon as the subject of change is brought up.

There's a saying from the movie *The Godfather* in which Michael Corleone says to Sonny, "It's not personal—it's business." The nature of the family business aside, these words came from a task-driven, stereotypical boss, whose only objective is to get the job done. But when the same line is raised in *You've Got Mail*, Kathleen Kelly debates this blanket statement with, "What is that supposed to mean? I am so sick of that. All that means is that it wasn't personal to you. But it was personal to me. It's personal to a lot of people."

The underlying meaning of the statement is that people take pride in their work. It is human nature to work toward and finish a task with a sense of accomplishment. From the time we were children shouting to our parents, "Look at me," throughout school when we work for high marks, the challenge to achieve and be recognized expands into adulthood, as we produce work that somehow contributes to society and earns us pay that is tied to our accomplishments. There is no humanly possible way to avoid taking these efforts personally. We're not fully immersed in the robotic age. Are we?

Now, add in the amount of time that is spent at our jobs. The eight-hour day is a myth within salaried professions. There is no denying we are a 24/7, global economy. This affects everything—from deadlines that have zero limitations to email notifications on our mobile phones, with no regard to time of day or day of the week. Throw on top of that an hour to two or even three in commuting, and employees are dedicating half of their lives to the job. Family photos line our desks to remember who we are doing this for, of course. But lunches, coffee, drinks, meetings, and retreats end up forging relationships that surpass family in a lot of ways because our coworkers speak our language, understand our pain points, and spend just as much (if not more) time with us. Even with the ability to tele-commute, this interwoven personal experience remains because tele-commuting has effectively allowed work to infiltrate home life—and once it does, it rarely turns back. So business is personal even if an employee knows it is not going to last forever.

Yet when change is presented to employees, it is often after the change pendulum has been swung. The plan is presented with the argument that change is what's best for the company, and if they're lucky, a personal encouragement or thank you is added at the end, while employees' minds are left to process the change announce-ment. From the employee standpoint, is it any wonder why most initial change reaction is discomforting? Again, I remind you, people don't hate change. They hate not having any say in it.

There are a few broad categories in the countless variations of possible, Initial Change Reaction scenarios. The variations are count-less, simply because everyone is different. Unless you are initiating change in a company that is completely driven by robots, there are no "one-approach-fits-all" implementations when it comes to intro-ducing corporate change. Even if a team shares the same role and responsibilities, not everyone on the team has the same emotional makeup or the same personal goals and circumstances. Any change, no matter how small, has the potential to impact an employee on both personal and professional levels, and this may generate conflict between existing values and beliefs.

For many reasons, the first key predictor of whether or not your company will successfully adapt to change is one of the biggest indi-cators of whether or not the new business practice will be a success. Initial Change Reaction can not only set the tone for the rest of the implementation, it can have huge implications for the company's reputation and standing in the business world. Imagine if I went to my supervisor and explained my grief over the limitations of not being able to participate in my team's change management project because I didn't have the word *manager* in my title, and it resulted in no change to the policy. A senior staff member, managing a team that was vital to introducing new revenue streams to a major corporation, is denied a chance at advancement and implementing improvements because of what equates to a human resources oversight. That alternative scenario could have cost the company one of their biggest champions of change. But remember, my initial reaction was very positive and, because of that, I was able to present my case to management so that I could get behind the new and improved direction the organization was heading.

The research is clear. The main reason change implementation of any scale fails is a lack of buy-in. So, the big question becomes how does one get genuine buy-in for important organizational changes, starting with the initial reaction to the announcement of change?

As a change manager, the first thing that must be understood is that every employee should not be treated the same—simply because everyone is different. In other words, people want to feel understood and that they are unique. Even if your business is a team of pillow stuffers, every one of them believes they are contributing a unique skill set to getting the stuffing inside to make a quality product.

It is not unfair to treat people differently, as long as it is in their best interest and it is mutually acceptable. For instance, someone's personal situation may require specific hours they can or cannot be in the office, that they discuss with you privately. This may at first seem unfair to other team members who have to work the "established" hours, but once explained, it is rare that the other members wouldn't calm down. In fact, working with an employee to develop an acceptable solution sends the message to others that, should personal circumstances arise that require flexibility, management will be open to discussing a workaround. Such sensitivity to the unique needs of employees demonstrates employee centricity, which is consistent with the teachings of stakeholder theory, one of the three theories this research was anchored on.

By holding targeted, one-on-one conversations, and paying attention to employee needs, you are much more likely to foster an initial positive reaction to change long before it is to be implemented. Listening to employees' lists of concerns, needs, and interests lets them know that they are valued members of the team. Then, when it comes time to ask for their commitment to what lies ahead, it becomes easier to announce the change, framed in a way that shows you listened, and that you will address their pain points, if not alleviate them. Getting buy-in by listening works much better than trying to sell them on your ideas because the change almost becomes employee-driven, and it makes you look like an understanding manager they will want to support.

Organizations do not need to wait until large-scale change is imminent to engage employees in work-life discussions. Rather, they should always be prepared for change by fostering an open exchange of ideas. In preparing, it is more natural to engage at the employee level. Consider the suggestion box effect. The presence of a tool that is for an employee of any rank to submit suggestions is a big motivator, and makes employees give more thought about how to make the workplace function better. One of the earliest examples of the workplace suggestion box came from the Japanese in 1721, when the eighth shogun, Yoshimuni Tokugawa, posted the following note: Make your idea known. Rewards are given for ideas that are accepted. In the hundreds of years since employee suggestion boxes, change has been a staple in organizational processes. There is a caveat to this approach. An empty suggestion box, or one that goes ignored by those who hold the key, equals an ineffective employee involvement program and is a sign of a toxic culture. Therefore, to avoid alienating employees, respond to suggestions you receive and use the ones you can.

Lastly, employees actively engaged in career-seeking behaviors are more likely to display supportive change behaviors than those who are more passive.[8] There are simple questionnaires available that

---

8   Lysova, E., Richardson, J., Khapova, S., & Jansen, P. (2015). Change-Supportive Employee Behavior: A Career Identity Explanation. Career Development International, 20(1). http://dx.doi.org/10.1108/CDI-03-2014-0042

can indicate a person's tendency to resist change, and this may be a good conversation starter to open the listening dialogue and gain support before implementing a change program that will require buy-in.[9]

Regardless of whether you have a merger coming up next year, or an internal shift is in the early planning stages, the time to institute methodologies that will foster a positive initial change reaction was yesterday. It is never too soon to prepare your staff to positively react to change. Initial change reaction is a proactive predictor, no matter how many different personalities are within your ranks. How? Initial change reaction is almost always driven by an employee's personal experiences. You, your management team and/or your human resources team, should know your employees well enough to understand what makes them tick on a professional *and* personal level. What drives them to want to get out of bed every morning and come to work? Once they get to work, what are their habits? Most importantly, what are their pain points during work?

What if your change involves a departmental move to another building? The new location may even be on the same street as the building the department is currently reporting to—but this new location is on the *other* side of the street, where traffic flows the other way. And maybe one team member is part of a ride share that continues on in the direction of the old location's side of the street. So, this person now has to cross a busy street to get to the new building. This can take another fifteen minutes, depending on traffic. Every minute she is late not only holds up other members of her project team, but her self-imposed pressure stresses her out so much that it takes another half an hour for her to be fully engaged in what she's supposed to be doing—*and* the added stress has strained her personal life and upped her blood pressure medication. Now, a seemingly innocent office move has turned into a massive nightmare—and this

---

9   Oreg, S. (2003). Resistance to change: Developing an individual differences measure. The Journal of Applied Psychology, 88(4), 680–963. doi:10.1037/0021-9010.88.4.680. Oreg resistance to change scale test: http://pluto.huji.ac.il/~oreg/questionnaire.php

is just for one person. Never underestimate the need to get the day started in a good mood.

This example may seem like such a small blip in the grand scheme of a billion-dollar acquisition, but that one blip may be happening to the person who is most revered among his peers. And for every blip, there are hundreds, if not thousands, of more seemingly small personal nuisances that can derail a company's day-to-day operation and ingrain a feeling of cynicism and resentment. Managers need not pry into an employee's personal life, but they do need to be aware of personal circumstances that can affect an employee's day and productivity.

As you seek to understand personal motivators and pain points when implementing change, be sure to consider how the individual choices an employee makes—in regards to the new structure—affects the rest of the team. Your employees may not all be best friends, but chances are, if they are in a position to be greatly affected by change implementation, then they've been with the company long enough to have established friendly relationships. So when communicating the rationale for change, it is also important to steal a little from George Bailey's story in the film *It's a Wonderful Life* by showing them the consequences of their reaction and involvement in the newly-changed structure, and what would happen if they were no longer there.

"Here are your choices and here are the consequences to the organization, your team and you, for each choice." Knowing the impact of their choices in accepting the change increases buy-in because it removes uncertainty. Employees know what will happen depending on what they choose to do. Removing uncertainty removes the main contributor to fear.

This cause and effect outline often leads to a human's desire to do what's right. Knowing, finding, or triggering that feeling of integrity within each individual creates a powerful attitude toward change that they can comfortably own.

Some fields are naturally more driven by analytics, and it pays for change managers to do a buy-in analysis. The right kind of key stakeholder commitment could be the tipping point of a successful model. By first examining the key stakeholders' reaction and determining if they are actively resisting change, letting the change happen, helping the change happen or making the change happen, change managers can get an early indication of how the levels of buy-in from senior staff will affect the reaction of the general employee base. Note that this is just a directional indicator, as junior staff will view the change from a different perspective and may react differently. Now, change managers can determine where the company *needs* the key stakeholder buy-in to be, and adjust the change implementation to reach the goal of what will make the change successful. This early buy-in analysis allows executive management to know what is most important to hold their ground on and what they have some flexibility with. Additionally, an early buy-in analysis provides the data to ensure the right people are brought in, at the right time, to ensure success.

The simplest way to generate buy-in for any level of employee is to create a shared vision of what the desired destination will look like. Envisioning the desired end goal begins by identifying pain points of today, and showing how the future will take care of the pain—or better, remove it completely. This type of "before and after" snapshot is the first step in gaining buy-in. Everyone desires to wish away some of their current problems, but there would, no doubt, be naysayers of this "pie-in-the-sky" picture. It is important not to crush the cynics. In fact, some of the best solutions may come from those who are willing to look at the end state as less than ideal.

I noticed that research into employee response during large-scale change execution in the pharmaceutical industry was lacking, in spite of the high-risk nature of the industry, and the myriad of consequences of poor change execution. For example, a drug costs $1.8 billion from discovery to commercialization with newer estimates as high as $2.5 billion.[10] This expensive, heavily regulated, and lengthy drug development process is an example of what drives companies

---

[10] Golec, J., Hegde, S., & Vernon, J. (2009). Pharmaceutical R&D spending and threats of price regulation. Journal of Financial and Quantitative Analysis, 45(1), 239. doi:10.1017/S0022109009990512

to merge. My study was designed to understand and document employee reactions that indicate their level of reaction to change, or support of the change, but the results are applicable to any scale of change implementation, across any type of business. Because, as you will see, I looked at how to manage change successfully from the ground up, rather than the top down, with a foundation in statistical analysis and quantitative, scientific research methods.

My study data is further supported by the wealth of change management studies done for other industries. Two components consistently rise to the top in all of the studies I looked at. 1) Employee participation in change is a key factor in effective and successful change management. 2) One of the most common negative outcomes of change is the costly consequence of losing talented employees, or worse, keeping them at half the focus required to succeed. This consequence leads to a logical solution of focusing on the people of the organization in a change initiative to facilitate success. Although this comes off as completely logical, most often, there simply aren't enough human resources to manage change from a people perspective, and the realities of employee and employer collide.

3 Collision of Employer and Employee Realities

Why does a great endeavor "take a village?"

A key driver of my study and this book is geared toward avoiding one of the most common negative outcomes of change: the costly consequence of losing talented employees, or keeping employees that are only partially engaged. We've discussed the dollar figure of consequences of employee turnover, but one source of value is much harder to compute. Since every employee is unique, each brings a unique perspective to the task they perform. Over time, their combined perspectives and diversity in thought strengthen the skill set of each team member and becomes a value to the business. When they leave, either on their own or through change implementation, they are taking that value with them, and most often it goes to the competition.

Change initiatives have not traditionally focused on the people involved as the primary target for implementation, because corporate change is a target with two halves: the employee half and the employer half. However, it is the employer who is responsible for approving the change, so it is looked at from their perspective first. The result, in many cases, turns out to be a collision in the middle when it should be a joining of two halves to make a better whole.

Recent studies have shown that the manner and the degree to which employees are included in change implementation enhance their organization's successful transition to a new working reality.

When we consider the basis that change implementation involves communication of new processes, and in some cases training on these processes, it makes perfect sense that those who are on the receiving end of the communication and training will be more receptive the more they are involved in developing the new standards.

Large-scale changes, such as mergers and acquisitions, are strategic events that usually include several proprietary and confidential elements. This poses a communication challenge to senior management who may not be authorized to share many aspects of the change freely. This reality makes it difficult to incorporate employee involvement in the decision to implement change.

Researchers Whelan-Berry and Somerville, observed that while change leaders of an organization may have a clear vision of change, they might not have considered whether the organization was ready for a change. They further observed that change leaders often did not consider how they might measure successful change afterward. In the end, they contended that while organizational change can be challenging and complex, it is also mappable and foreseeable.[11]

When poorly executed, major organizational changes (such as mergers and acquisitions) are often disruptive, costly to organizations, and sometimes demoralizing to employees. The results of my study, as it relates to the pharmaceutical industry, provide practical implications that support guiding the creation of a supportive work environment during organizational change—a transitional environment in which employees are motivated and engaged in their jobs to meet health and medical needs globally, all while the companies create skilled jobs and generate profit. These practical implications are made possible by analyzing the four key predictors of whether employees are likely to support change:

- *Initial change reaction.* Participants' responses when first learning about organizational change, as either negative or

---

[11] Whelan-Berry, K., and Somerville, K. (2010). Linking change drivers and the organizational change process: A review and synthesis. Journal of Change Management, 10(2), 175–193. doi:10.1080/14697011003795651

positive, ranging from "I will lose my job," to "I will get promoted."

- *Perceived change success.* The degree to which employees perceive a proposed change as completely and effectively implemented.
- *Involvement in change development.* The degree to which an employee takes part in the planning and implementation of change.
- *Change communication.* The timing, frequency, and quality of communication of the plan, its progress and its result.

We know how important initial change reaction can be, but overall, there are degree to which an employee will embrace (or reject) change implementation:[12]

- *Active Resistance.* Opposing the change through clear and deliberate actions.
- *Passive resistance.* Subtle, inconspicuous actions intended to oppose a change.
- *Compliance.* Demonstrating minimum support for change by acquiescing to change, but doing so reluctantly.
- *Cooperation.* Demonstrating support for change by putting forth effort in change initiatives, and being willing to make modest sacrifices.
- *Championing.* An extreme enthusiasm for change and doing more than is formally required to ensure change success, and promoting the change to others.

Before we look at each individual predictor, it is important to have a baseline of the many variables that can influence reaction and the support (or lack thereof) that follows during implementation. I approached employee involvement in change as a multidimen-

---

[12] Herscovitch, L., & Meyer, J. (2002). Commitment to Organizational Change: Extension of a Three-Component Model. *Journal of Applied Psychology* 87(3), 474–487. doi:10.1037//0021-9010.87.3.474

sional construct, similar to the approach Herscovitch and Meyer took,—where compliance, cooperation, and championing encompass the range of employee support from minimal support of change to enthusiastic promotion or championing of change; the negative aspects of response to change, active, and passive resistance complete the continuum of reaction to change.[13]

Sometimes employees do not have strong opinions about organizational change, and their lack of response could be misinterpreted. Failing to consider ambivalence can lead to misrepresentation of employees' reactions to change. In addition, employee reaction to change is not unidirectional, and employees' feelings about management can influence their reaction.[14]

To further complicate matters, employees can both resist and support aspects of the same change, and those employees' personal attitudes toward change interact with their attitudes toward the change agent, which can result in ambivalence. Even employees with a positive impression of the change agent could still be ambivalent to organizational change.

It was inevitable that I would come across instances where change met some active resistance. While it is easy to grasp that not every employee will jump aboard the change bandwagon, it is curious as to what would make someone expend their efforts, actively resisting a change initiative as opposed to supporting it, even if it means the most minimal support, which is basic compliance.

To investigate this further, let's take a look at change management theory. Change management theory falls under the umbrella of organizational and social psychology and is associated with Lewin's[15]

---

[13] Herscovitch, L., and Meyer, J. (2002). Commitment to Organizational Change: Extension of a Three-Component Model. *Journal of Applied Psychology,* 87(3), 474–487. doi:10.1037//0021-9010.87.3.474

[14] Oreg, S., and Sverdlik, N. (2011). Ambivalence toward imposed change: The conflict between dispositional resistance to change and the orientation toward the change agent. *The Journal of Applied Psychology,* 96(2), 337–349. doi:10.1037/a0021100.

[15] Frontiers of group dynamics: Concept, method and reality in social science; social equilibria, and social change. *Human Relations, 1*(5), 5–41

ideas on change processes and group dynamics. Lewin, who is often recognized as the founder of social psychology, developed a 3-stage model of the change process that describes moving from a position of stasis into a new position or perspective. These stages of change consist of unfreezing (the undoing of an established mindset or approach), actual change (which involves a certain degree of uncertainty about the future), and freezing (the establishment of a new mindset or position).

Researchers have also found that the mode of change management influenced employee experiences of change: positive experiences resulted from informal, relational techniques, while negative experiences largely resulted from more formal, authoritative managerial techniques. Human resource managers were selected based on technical expertise, rather than on relational skills, so when change arrived, managers did not have the relational or team building skills to effectively usher their teams down new paths.[16]

When it came to how well employees identified with their leadership, and how supportive of innovation the organization was in relation to its employees, the research shows that the interaction of all three parameters (leadership style, the climate of innovation, and identification with leader) fostered employee creativity. The researchers focused on a large number of organizations across multiple industries, including pharmaceutical companies.

Pharmaceutical company employees must follow strict protocols to comply with a multitude of regulations associated with research involving human subjects. However, tremendous room exists for creativity and innovation relating to process improvement to accelerate drug development. Therefore, change management practices that support the interaction of these three elements could have a positive effect on employee reaction to change in this otherwise regimented industry.

---

[16] Barratt-Pugh, Bahn, and Gakere (2013) studied organization change associated with the merger of two dissimilar state government departments in Western Australia.

There remains an opportunity to optimize change management effects in an innovative, transformational leadership environment, where employees identify with leaders. Transformational leaders often bring about desired effects through inspirational motivation, personal charisma, and by considering and motivating followers. In a business environment where the main motivation is to make a profit, owners (including shareholders) have been seen as the primary stakeholder, and many business decisions are made based on the interests of this particular level of stakeholder. However, the interests and concerns of other parties involved, with stakes in an enterprise, should matter as well when making business decisions. According to the theory, this inclusive approach creates ownership and a sense of belonging for those involved. Like transformational leadership, stakeholder theory relies on a bottom-up approach that has the potential to engage crucial stakeholders, such as employees, in the change process.[17]

Much like grief, when we lose someone or something dear, with change, there are phases to grow through this often-difficult transition. With transition theory, our perception of the situation could be escalating in "severity" of impact and importance to our sense of self, as we go through the phases of dealing with change. We descend into the trough of depression via a small impact on our sense of self (anxiety about what this means on a personal level), speed up through a greater realization of impact and meaning (fear, threat) and then comes the realization that, potentially, our core sense of self has been impacted, and our "self-belief system" undermined to a large extent (guilt, depression), which contradicts who we thought we were. Chances are most human resources teams aren't thinking along these lines as they walk employees through the plan.

Now, if someone is going through multiple transitions at the same time, these will have a cumulative impact on them as individuals. Some could be going through all the different transitions almost simultaneously. This is most evident at the middle manage-

---

[17] Freeman, R. (1984). Strategic management: A stakeholder approach. Boston, MA: Pittman.

ment level. For instance, in my case, I was considered a leader and I knew the change was needed. But suddenly, I found my ego bruised and I was disappointed and uncertain. In scenarios like this, it then becomes a case of assessing accumulated "evidence", some of which may support a previous negative experience; and the influence of that experience can evolve into a rapid dropping of self-confidence and increasing negative self-image. We end up similar to a deer, frozen in the headlights, not knowing which way to turn or who to trust.

It is important to consider and agree on the expectation of what the change implementation will look like. To managers or shareholders, the change in the bottom line is key. But to employees, change in productivity, responsibility or quality of work environment are the pain triggers. So, while something may be visible on the spreadsheet, on the ground it may be imperceptible, and vice-versa.

Findings from interviews and surveys of employees of a Philippine property and development firm confirmed that employees who experienced poor change management in the past are inclined to react poorly to new changes.[18] More specifically, the researchers found that poor change management history led to decreased openness to change, job satisfaction, and trust, as well as to increased cynicism and turnover intentions. There go the valuable employees, again. The findings of this study had significant implications for the pharmaceutical industry. The frequency of organizational change in the pharmaceutical industry suggests that there is a good chance pharmaceutical employees and companies have experienced, or will experience, change—making the consideration of poor change management history on individual and organizational levels important to change implementation and management. The same can be said for larger companies in many sectors that are constantly evolving, such as media, technology, energy, and finance.

---

[18] Bordia, P., Restubog, S., Jimmieson, N., & Irmer, B. (2011). Haunted by the past: Effects of poor change management history on employee attitudes and turnover. Group & Organization Management, 36(2), 191–222. http://dx.doi.org/10.1177/1059601110392990

Causality is a frame of reference for connecting people and phenomena; a framework that attributes causes of behavior to self and others.[19] Broadly speaking, causality is the principle that everything has a cause. When it comes to predicting change reaction, interpretations of an individual's framework enable us to predict or infer what behaviors or events are likely to occur based on their causality frameworks. In other words, an individual's framework is based on previous experiences and beliefs that help forecast the possible reactions and behaviors. Again, these variables come with multi-dimensional factors to consider.

Employees as stakeholders: Organizations strive to ensure that stakeholders, such as board members and investors who make significant contributions to the organization's financial success, are treated well. Other stakeholders, such as junior employees whose contributions may not be as closely and directly linked to the company's success, can be neglected unless the organization makes deliberate efforts to account for them. This framework suggests that, at lower hierarchical levels, important contributions employees make to a change's success may be neglected or may be missed entirely.[20] Remember that low man holding up the totem pole? This is why he's often on shaky ground.

Emotional dimensions of employee commitment to change: Emotional dissonance is the difference between, say, a sales representative's true feelings and the positive expression the representative must display to customers—even if the representative's true feelings are negative. In a 2010 study, Mishra and Bhatnagar looked at linking emotional dissonance and organizational identification to turnover intention.[21] They found, through hierarchical regression

[19] Valence refers to an individual's evaluation of the significance of an event or a relationship.

[20] Greenwood, M., & Buren III, H. (2010). Trust and stakeholder theory: Trustworthiness in the organization–stakeholder relationship. Journal of Business Ethics, 95(3), 425–438. doi:10.1007/s10551-010-0414-4

[21] Mishra, S. & Bhatnagar, D. (2010). Linking emotional dissonance and organizational identification to turnover intention and emotional well-being: A study of medical representatives in India. Human Resource Management, 49(3), 401–419. doi:10.1002/hrm http://onlinelibrary.wiley.com/doi/10.1002/

analysis, that this emotional conflict, or dissonance, was a predictor of employee turnover intentions. By now you are probably seeing a pattern as to why companies lose so much value with employee turnover. In addition, the study found that an employee's need to display potentially opposite emotions about what they were feeling was a significant source of employee dissatisfaction. In other words, they felt guilty about having to put up a false front for the sake of the company. They also found that organizational identification and commitment were not always matters of outright support or resistance, and that organizational identification and commitment to change are complex and sometimes ambivalent.

Coping with change and turnover intentions are related to commitment to change. Affective commitment may increase when employees participate in the change process, as involvement helps them cope with change.[22]

Locus of control refers to a person's perception of their ability to exercise control over contextual elements of a situation, and, by now, we know that it's not change people hate, it's their lack of control over it. In locus of control, individuals are referred to as being either internals or externals. Those who consider themselves internal believe they have control over their situations (i.e., that the locus of control is within them), and those who consider themselves external believe that situational factors control their lives (i.e., that the locus of control resides outside of them).[23]

Those with high internal locus of control showed higher affective and normative commitment to change than those with high external locus of control did. But those with high external locus of control were higher in continuance commitment to change. The

---

hrm.20362/abstract;jsessionid=6F2743B066159830AD7F70179DE16409.f02t02

[22] Cunningham, G. (2006). The relationships among commitment to change, coping with change, and turnover intentions. European Journal of Work and Organizational Psychology, 15(1), 29–45. doi:10.1080/13594320500418766

[23] Herscovitch, L., & Meyer, J. (2002). Commitment to organizational change: Extension of a three-component model. Journal of Applied Psychology, 87(3), 474–487. doi:10.1037//0021-9010.87.3.474

conclusion of this is that those who believe they have control over their situation commit to change out of personal desire (affective) or obligation, while those who believe the control is outside of them commit to change because of their perception of the costs associated with failure to support change.[24]

Reflecting on the responses on the change continuum, ranging from active resistance to championing change, only 5.1% of the participants fell in the championing change category (See figure 1). This 5.1% is an interesting result because the four independent variables predicted championing, indicating that when employees display the most enthusiastic, supportive change behaviors, the change is likely to be successful—provided other aspects of the change are proceeding well.

---

[24] Chen, J., & Wang, L. (2007). Locus of control and the three components of commitment to change. Personality and Individual Differences, 42(3), 503–512. doi:10.1016/j.paid.2006.07.025

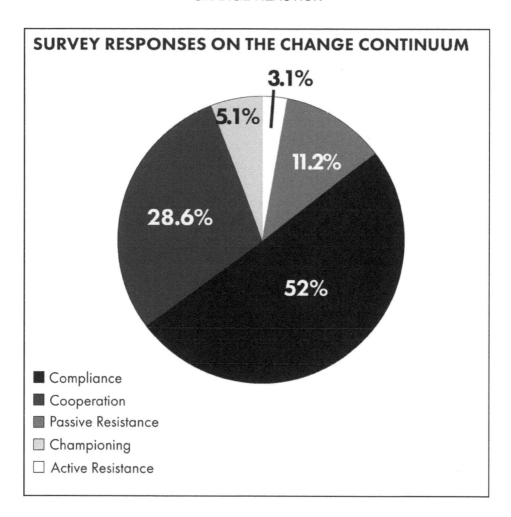

Figure 1: SURVEY RESPONSES ON CHANGE CONTINUUM

Major change initiatives are usually initiated in response to internal and external pressures. Organizations merge and remove management layers in response to challenging economic climates. This need for change or adaptation has been compared to that of a burning platform.[25]

---

[25] Fletcher, G. (2009). Escaping burning platforms. Manufacturing Engineering, 143(5), 104. http://www.sme.org/manufacturingengineering

Change initiatives have not traditionally focused on people as the primary target. Regardless of the change rationale, change model, philosophy, and selected change management tools, the emphasis of change initiatives is usually directed at specific processes or products.[26]

Of the participants in my study, only 3.1% described themselves as having actively resisted change, and only another 11.2% passively resisted change. Although it is possible that respondents to this type of survey were those more likely to support change, organizations should be encouraged by the low percentage of employees who resist change. This finding creates an opportunity for organizations to leverage the fact that the vast majority of employees support change. What is more interesting, however, is that of those who supported change, a majority (60.7%) only comply with it (provide minimal support). Organizations can create a more targeted approach to change management that could identify and help convert some employees passively resisting change, and move the compliant employees up the reaction to change continuum, making them more supportive of change.

---

[26] Pellissier, R. (2011). The implementation of resilience engineering to enhance organizational innovation in a complex environment. International Journal of Business and Management, 6(1), 145–164. http://dx.doi.org/10.5539/ijbm.v6n1p145

Managers hold more loyalty than companies

A concept map can be used to demonstrate the consequences of two influencers of manager reaction to change for both communication and stakeholder engagement. The concept map (*Figure 2*) implies that frequent communication and stakeholder engagement result in positive manager reaction to change.

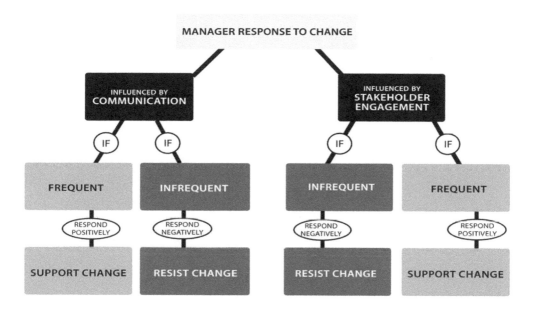

Figure 2: CONCEPT MAP OF MANAGER REACTION TO CHANGE

Teamwork is about helping each other through the process as effectively as possible. This is where the answer to "why a great endeavor takes a village" comes in. The team effort is particularly important as it relates to each person experiencing transition through variants at slightly different speeds[27], and quite possibly at different places on different paths—depending on just what is happening to them at the time (*Figure 4*).

Much of the speed of transition will depend on the individual's self-perception, the locus of control, and other past experiences, and how these all combine to create their anticipation of future events. The more positive you see the outcome, the more control you have (or believe you have) over both the process and the final result; and the less difficult and negative a journey everyone will have.

A slight shift in key factors can tip the reaction and speed of transition to change. This is what we know about how people relate to change.

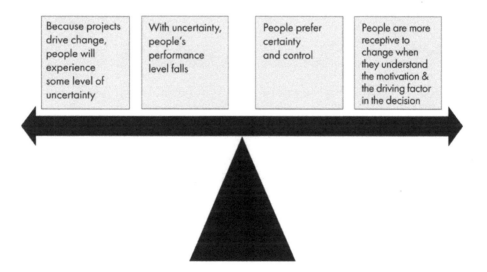

Figure 3: THE BALANCING ACT OF CONTROL

---

[27] Fischer (2012) The Personal Transition Curve; Originally presented at the Tenth International Personal Construct Congress, Berlin, 1999, and subsequently developed in his work on constructivist theory in relation to service provision organizations at Leicester University, England, John Fisher's model of personal change - The Personal Transition Curve - revised again in Nov 2012

A concept map is used here (*Figure 4*) to show the rollercoaster-like wave of transition to change variances.

Concept Map of Transition Variances

Figure 4: TRANSITION VARIANCES

Transition variances can go from complacency to hostility in a short period of time.

Anxiety. Can I cope?

Happiness. It's about time.

Fear. How does this affect me?

Threat. This is bigger than I thought and there's no turning back.

Denial. Nothing is changing.

Depression. This isn't for me.

Hostility. I make my own change or I'll make this work if it kills me.

Gradual acceptance. I can see myself in the future—this may just work.

Champion of the new way. Look at the impressive results already.

Part 2

The 4 Key Predictors of Reaction and Consequences to Change

Recent studies have shown that the manner and the degree to which employees are included in change implementation enhances their organization's successful transition to a new working reality.[28] I addressed the lack of knowledge and understanding about employee response to change by examining whether any of the four factors (initial change reaction, change communication, involvement in change development, and perceived change success) predict employee response to large-scale change initiatives. This study was also designed to provide practical information on employee response to change to inform pharmaceutical managers and associated change leaders who are planning and implementing change.

Again, here are the specific factors that I investigated:

- *Change communication.* The timing, frequency, and quality of communication of the plan, its progress and its result.
- *Initial change reaction.* Participants' responses when first learning about organizational change as either negative or positive, ranging from: "I will lose my job", to "I will get promoted."
- *Involvement in change development.* The degree to which an employee takes part in the planning and implementation of change.
- *Perceived change success.* The degree to which employees perceive a proposed change as completely and effectively implemented.

Employee support was measured in terms of compliance, cooperation, and championing, and represent varying degrees of positive response to change. The negative response was categorized as either passive or active resistance. Knowledge of these factors is crucial for developing effective change management strategies that mitigate the potentially disruptive effects on employees and business operations.

---

[28] Gallup Research: The Gallup Path to Business Performance

4 Predictor 1: Change Communication

Effective communication is 20% what you know
and 80% how you feel about what you know.
—Jim Rohn

The first step in preparing for and implementing change is to explain it. Change communication refers to the manner in which management conveys information relevant to the proposed change to employees, as well as the frequency and substance during follow-up information sharing. Change communication involves the clarity and quality of communication, where "Very bad" = 1, and "Very good" = 7. Frequency described how often the change was communicated to employees, and ranged from "Rarely" = 1, to "Very often" = 7.

I calculated the change communication score as the average of these two measures. Thus, this variable ranged from 1 to 7, where higher scores corresponded with a frequent, high-quality level of communication about the change.

The population studied was comprised of pharmaceutical industry employees with various years of experience. These individuals worked at traditional pharmaceutical companies that discover and develop investigational medicinal products (IMPs). The participants also worked at biotechnology companies that discover IMPs, but outsource development to contract research organizations, which were also a population of interest.

In order to be eligible, the participants must have also experienced some large-scale change in their company, such as a merger and acquisition. This change had to have occurred at their current employer or at a previous organization where the participant worked (*Figure 5*). Through my survey tool, I ensured targeting of a diverse sample representing various levels of experience and job categories, including change management experts.

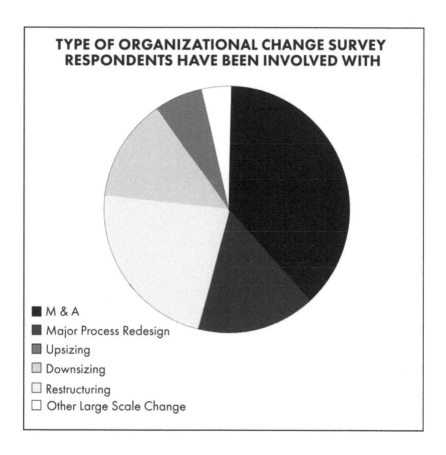

Figure 5: RESPONDENTS INVOLVEMENT
IN ORGANIZATIONAL CHANGE

I selected the factors evaluated in my study because previous researchers found that one or more of these factors predicted employee response to change, and led to change success in other industries. These industries included law enforcement (Ford et al., 2003), the hospitality industry (Hartline & Ferrell, 1996), the electronics industry (Goksoy et al., 2012), and the publishing industry Franckeiss (2012). In a 2012 study of a global, print-based publishing company that was transitioning to digital formats, Franckeiss found that various hands-on change inclusion techniques and frequent change communication through webinars before, during, and after change implementation increased change success. My results weren't identical. Rather, what I found was that none of the four predictors studied proved to be able to predict the success of change implementation—individually. They have to be considered together with the other 3 factors I shared in this book. The results, therefore, support the theory that change is multidimensional and best examined through multidimensional approaches.

Generating Employee Commitment and Support of Change

Employee commitment to and support of change has been the subject of extensive research.[29] Effective organizational change management is crucial to how organizations successfully handle large-scale change, and employee participation in and support of change are key factors in successful change initiatives. Getting employees to commit to new procedures, policies, and goals involving change, increases the likelihood of change success.[30] This commitment implies that employees will support the change. Multidimensional components

---

[29] Lau, C., & Woodman, R. (1995). Understanding organizational change: A schematic perspective. Academy of Management Journal, 38, 537–554. http://dx.doi.org/10.2307/256692

[30] Jaros, S. (2010). Commitment to organizational change: A critical review. Journal of Change Management, 10(1), 79–108. doi:10.1080/14697010903549457

of employee response involve behavioral and attitudinal components as well as emotional ones.

However, it all starts with communication. When asked about the communication leading up to the change initiative, on a scale where 1= "It was the worst," and 7= "It could not have been better", more than 22% responded with a 1. The next highest percentage landed right in the middle, which tends to be a "safe bet." Even more interesting to me was that only 4% responded with "the best," or a rating of 7. This data indicates that employees generally have a negative perception of change communication, and feel that the quality and frequency of change communication is usually poor.

The goal of a change agent is to help make the transition as effective and painless as possible. This goal is achieved by providing education, information, support, and by listening to and addressing questions. To perform these activities well, a change agent needs to be approachable and easy to talk to.

During a merger, it is important to acknowledge the concerns of all key stakeholders and treat them fairly. However, being overly polite can prevent sound data collection and optimal decision-making. It is ironic that politeness has been found to hinder change progress. Let's use a couple-counseling session to illustrate this point.

A couple seeks out counseling because they have a problem they are unable to handle on their own. Without close scrutiny, one would think that all is well between the couple because they are always so polite to each other. On close examination, however, the politeness is awkward and unstable. Whenever the lady makes a statement that appears to place blame on the man, she looks at him as if to ask, "I wasn't too harsh on you. Was I?" The lady also avoids eye contact with her boyfriend, except for those awkward, validation-seeking glances.

The boyfriend and counselor also have an unstable, polite demeanor. The boyfriend responds to most comments by first agreeing with his girlfriend or acknowledging that her point is valid. He then, almost passively, states his dissatisfaction with his girlfriend's commitment to the relationship based on her reluctance to assume his last name. The counselor, as expected, takes great care not to offend or take side with either party. As such, she tries to get them to respond to each other's concerns so she would continue to appear impartial to them.

In a high-pressure merger situation, this kind of patience and politeness may not be possible, and most likely would get in the way of progress. This isn't to suggest that communication needs to be rude, or even blunt, in order to make progress—but it does have to be honest. Change is uncomfortable.

When it comes to change communication, it is important to keep feedback and discussion frequent and ongoing, just as expected in the normal work environment. The thing about communicating that seems the most obvious, but is often the most overlooked, is the fact that in order for communication to be effective, or produce a desired response or action, it has to be a two-way event. During change implementation, don't wait for an annual or bi-annual review cycle. Provide feedback to team members in real-time and as often as possible; and be open to feedback in real-time as well. This is crucial to giving employees that sense of control that comes with being involved in the change that is affecting them. Two-way communication will foster a collaborative sentiment within the company, and help people see that things are running smoothly and on-task. Additionally, employees are often more productive and happy when they're being recognized for the good work they're doing.[31] If you can measure it, reward it. When milestones are celebrated, people will strive to excel at them.

Regardless of how many times we hear that "it's not personal, it's business," the effect of any change starts by being personal. Employees' first reaction, whether good, bad or indifferent, is always based on how they think the announcement will impact their day-to-day life.

Avoid a "one-size-fits-all" approach to communicating change. During organizational change, it is particularly important to custom-

---

[31] Manish Sood, CEO and founder of data-driven applications company Reltio, quoted in Inc. Magazine: http://www.inc.com/christina-desmarais/the-daily-habits-of-21-highly-successful-people.html

ize and target messages to meet the needs of the different employee groups within your organization. Occasionally, such targeting may require management to get personal in order to tailor the change appropriately, which can create another set of problems.

Too much mixing of business objectives with personal desires can lead to the old mantra, "familiarity breeds contempt." But at the same time, it is important to show employees that you are human and that you realize they are too. How does a manager find the right balance? Finding the answer and solution starts with communication. Let's say you have an employee, John, who produces good results, but is usually or always calling in sick. The other team members like John, but are often frustrated and held up by his absence and lateness. You're close enough with John that you can go to his house for dinner, but you don't want to interfere with his personal life. You can't let it continue as you're more than a little put off by the fact that John hasn't explained what's going on. Soon, rumors start circulating, you're growing frustrated, other team members start underperforming, and the original offender has become somewhat guarded and paranoid because he thinks everyone has been staring at him.

This is classic communication breakdown, which could be avoided by simply asking John why he has trouble adhering to the established work schedule. By keeping your questions short and un-accusatory, the employee is not on the defensive and has the option to share as much as they feel is needed. You can then notify the rest of the team of John's adjusted schedule, so they do not assume that he is simply breaking the rules with no explanation. In fact, by opening the communication door with a simple question, and exercising flexibility to the unique needs of your employee, you get to stay in the "good guy" category and remain the one who can more easily introduce change when needed.

In announcing organizational change initiatives, especially those as large as a merger or acquisition, organizations must be careful in communicating the right type and amount of information. Although all affected parties can benefit from a general overview of the change, each stakeholder or category of stakeholders will need more information on specific aspects of the change they deem more relevant to them. As such, the organization should create a change communication plan that addresses this need. Figure 6 is an example of the "diversity in information" needs related to a contemplated change.

STAKEHOLDER	TYPE	INFORMATION NEED
Managers	Primary	Intended business benefits and resources needed
Employees who execute the process	Primary	Reason for change in process and detailed procedures
Process management head or change management professional	Primary	Realization metrics and scope of change
Other functional areas	Secondary	Awareness of process change
External clients	Secondary	Awareness of process change components that affect interactions with them

Figure 6: STAKEHOLDER INFORMATION NEEDS ANALYSIS

At all levels, stakeholders want to know what will stay the same, what will go away and what will be new. For anything that changes, they will want to know the effect on their day-to-day existence. Here are a few tips to help with these information needs.

- Begin the dialogue with an explanation of the reason or motivation for the change. This is a natural way to start the conversation, but follow with specific details, as employees will need a real reason to hang onto. A tangible reason could be that the organization's revenue has dropped over the last few quarters, or a key drug is about to go off-patent with no strong backup in the pipeline.

- During change, pre-schedule information sharing sessions to ensure that employees hear about changes at the same time, or immediately after you advise the market or the media.
- Equip managers with additional information, so they can, in turn, support their staff. Too often, we instruct employees to go to their managers with questions, yet the managers know nothing more than what was shared with the employees.
- Tap into the tone of employee conversations by listening and observing twice as much as speaking. Employees have good insights into how the change will affect operations at the lowest levels. Why not hear what they have to say? They may suggest a small adjustment that could make the difference between success and failure.

Whenever you're conveying information that may be perceived as bad news, you should assume that your staff might already be discussing it. Change management involves setting the record straight, and providing an opportunity for interaction and discussion. Not only should you communicate the news quickly and honestly, you should also pinpoint and address employee concerns.

The best way of communicating change, especially news of an impending crisis, is face-to-face—even if that means video conferencing. A company-wide meeting, or department-wide session, should be among the communication vehicles. You should provide opportunities for a question-and-answer session. If you think some employees will be afraid to speak up, which is often the case, let them submit questions anonymously.

Whatever you do, don't ignore bad news. By not addressing tough situations, you risk exacerbating the problem. In changing times, you cannot over-communicate. If you fail to address the situation, rumors will spiral. Remember that one of the most important rules of change management is that employees want to know not only what's happening in the company, but also why it's happening.

When employees feel unsure, they may clam up or communicate rumors. Discussion forums let them post their concerns. So, when a leader stands in front of an audience of employees and talks about how much he welcomes their input about ways to implement change, the message gets derailed if that executive hides behind a lectern, and never faces the very people he or she is asking for support.

It is human nature to second-guess, and "not-so-good" rumors may run rampant along the company grapevine without enough information to prevent the spread. To mitigate, clearly communicate the vision, mission, and objectives. Help people understand how these changes will affect them personally, and the steps being taken to make sure the change is as seamless as possible. The more information you give, the less uncertainty and anxiety there will be. The less you share, the more misconceptions, which will most likely be more negative than positive. Lack of communication is one of the biggest complaints employees have toward their manager. Be known as the manager who over-communicates, rather than under-communicates. This will also help build trust in you as a leader.

You can either talk to everyone at the same time, or each individually. Here are some guidelines to follow:

> Create a roadmap and discuss it. Include not only how everyone will get from point A to point B, but also communicate what point A, is. It is important to start off with everyone's understanding of the current state. That way, there is something to measure point B against.

The Milestones of a Change Communication Roadmap

A) SITUATION

Analyze where you are as an organization, as a department, and as an individual. In this process, don't just state the obvious. Get into what works well and what could use improvement, as well as how the change may affect the current state.

B) OBJECTIVES and MOTIVATION

State what the objective of the change is. Filter this information based on priority if necessary, in order to avoid information overload. Say why the change is needed. Explain how the change will result in a better situation for the company and its stakeholders, especially employees.

C) THE TAKEAWAY MESSAGE

It is essential to frame your communication in a way that supports the overall objective. As new ideas emerge while shaping the change initiative, seek opportunities to link these ideas to the overall key objective. That way, everyone remains focused. Craft the message in a way that resonates with employees, so they will have a reason to support the change. Do not just speak about earnings per share or use financial jargon that will not readily resonate.

D) PLAN AND PATH OF ACTION

Decide on the implementation strategy, and inquire if anyone has any suggestions or additional implementation solutions. Finally, select the most effective ways to keep everyone engaged and up to date during the change.

E) DEFINE SUCCESS

Even if the change is strictly a financial decision, it's imperative to communicate with those you are asking to change what the end game is, and how they will know if they achieved or realized the intended benefits of the change.

Communicate to everyone at the same time if:

- It is necessary for everyone to hear the news at the same time. This is not only as outlined in the stakeholder needs analysis in *Figure 6*, but also take into consideration how active your corporate grapevine is, or in some cases how closely media outlets are tuned into your company.
- You want to get your employees involved to generate ideas, and help in finding solutions to issues that may come up during implementation of the change. This is also a good way to create teamwork and ensure stakeholder engagement within the group.
- You want to briefly announce to everyone a major event, and then immediately follow up with individual and smaller team or department meetings.

Identify key people and communicate to each individually if:

- You anticipate that it will cause a high degree of emotion, which can be counter-productive.
- The subject matter is sensitive and can be considered private or embarrassing to these key individuals.
- The changes involve actions that should remain confidential. It might be related to pay, classification, employment status, or downsizing or the stock market.
- If you know there will be troublemakers in a full group setting that might make matters worse or confuse the message being delivered.

You can share the change information either verbally or in writing. In most cases, it is a good idea to use both written and verbal communication. A good rule of thumb is the more emotional the issue, the more it should be verbal rather than written. This is because written information is more likely to be misinterpreted, and tone does not come across if not carefully written.

Let your staff ask questions and provide honest answers. If you do not know the answer, it is better to say, "I don't know, but I will find out as soon as possible." Be sure to always follow up. Also, listen and don't be defensive. In most cases, the change will be out of your control so do not take complaints personally. Be sure you have said all that you have to say, and don't end the conversation until you have made the points perfectly clear. Do not just state the change as fact, and then quickly flee the scene. No matter the form of communication or the size of the audience these simple steps will help you form a plan:

1. Be clear and honest about what's changing and why.

     Any sort of spin, sugarcoating or jargon is going to look like you're trying to hide something. You'll gain employees' trust if you use simple, straightforward language, and are completely upfront about what's changing and why. Don't talk down to employees as it will make them feel resentful and unvalued. Some companies make the mistake of believing their employees can't handle the truth, but people respond well to respectful and honest communication.

2. Consider the emotional impact of the change.

     Organizational changes often strike a personal chord with employees. Suddenly the company is toying with their health care, and maybe that affects their sick child. Alternatively, a company may be implementing an outcome-based wellness program, which means employees have to make lifestyle changes they don't want to make. Take these concerns into consideration when crafting your message—and outright acknowledge them too. Sometimes people just need to feel heard.

3. Tell employees what's in it for them.

     It is the age-old marketing credo: What's In It For Me? You can't deny we're all looking out for Number 1, so hyping "good corporate citizenship" as a reason for the change is a waste of time. Explain the benefits of the change and what employees will get from it. Yes, things will be different—acknowledge that. Yes, everyone may not like what's changing—acknowledge that too. But there's generally an upside, so outline that as well. If there's no upside, then say so. Admit that what's happening is not ideal and talk about what you'll do to make the change as smooth as possible. Then thank employees for their patience, cooperation, ongoing contributions to the company and for sticking with you through the shift.

4. Explain how the change will happen.

Employees feel reassured and are more easily able to get on board when you paint a clear picture of what's going to happen and when. If you have to use a numbered step-by-step list, do it. If your employees respond well to graphics, use them. Just make sure to set expectations by explaining the process so people can clearly see the road ahead.

5. Tell employees what they need to do.

It is really the infamous call to action. It's critical to outline what needs to be done—and when. This is what people are looking for at the end of a communication. So use bulleted lists, bold font, links to websites, etc., to highlight the necessary action.

6. Consider the source – and the channels.

Change communications are generally best delivered from the top. Develop a cascading messaging strategy that starts with your CEO or another senior executive, and then encourage directors and managers to discuss the change in more detail with their teams. Make sure to use a variety of media: email, all-hands meetings, company intranet, home mailings (especially if family members are affected) and a frequently asked questions (FAQ) document for further details.

7. Target whenever you can.

    Give careful thought to specific audiences that are more affected by the change, either immediately or otherwise. For example, with healthcare changes, you may want to develop communications specific to families or those with chronic conditions. With a wellness program, consider how it will affect people who might have difficulty achieving the desired outcomes (like quitting smoking, losing weight or lowering blood sugar levels).

8. Open two-way communication channels.

    Remember employees needing to feel heard? Create two-way communication resources where they can ask questions, express their concerns and get answers. A dedicated email address is a great start, but a town hall (or series of them) goes one step further. It's more personal and—if you execute it right—will feel like, "We're all in this together." Allow employees to ask questions and address all of them—clearly and honestly.

There are two upsides to nearly every change initiative, but you need to plan ahead before the initial communication is started.

1. Empowerment nets commitment. By identifying roles and responsibilities that will need to be added as part of managing the change (not as a result of the actual change once it is implemented) when you announce it, you can solicit volunteers for these roles, and in doing so, increase the level of commitment.

2. Opportunity for growth or to try to do something different. Be prepared for employees that come to the realization that the change is a good reason to move on and, just maybe, they can move on within the new structure. In other words, the new business set up may allow an in-road for employees to take a position that would have raised some eyebrows during the "old way."

During the change implementation, it is useful to establish a network of change agents to solicit feedback from peers in informal settings. In a study of the merger of two state government departments in Western Australia, employees had a positive experience with change when change agents used informal, relational techniques. With the feedback from the informal interactions, change leaders can adjust aspects of the implementation plan to meet stakeholder needs more effectively. This network of change agents will address a critical need to acknowledge, and respond, to stakeholder concerns during change implementation. Incorporating feedback through this communication vehicle even after the major change decisions have been made can be a useful way to gain additional support for the change.[32]

Proper problem identification needs to be articulated in the initial change communication especially when the change is a result of a corporate crisis. Consider the magnitude of the BP oil spill. A company in this position has multiple problems and multiple decisions to make. How the CEO handles these problems and decisions is usually the subject of close public scrutiny as demonstrated by the detailed media coverage of this case. During the weeks and months following the initial incident, the media kept reporting an increased magnitude of the spill, which indicated that the company either did not understand the problem very well, or they were just being deceptive.

Assuming that BP had good intentions and was not being deceptive, they did a poor job of defining the problem. Consequently, they tried several failed options based on a lower estimate of the true magnitude of the spill. Not knowing the extent of the problem placed BP's CEO at a disadvantage.[33] Therefore, proper problem identification was the biggest step bypassed.

---

[32] Barratt-Pugh, L., Bahn, S., & Gakere, E. (2013). Managers as change agents: Implications for human resource managers engaging with culture change. Journal of Organizational Change Management, 26(4), 748–764. doi:10.1108/JOCM-Feb-2011-0014

[33] Stryker, P. (2001). How to analyze that problem: part II of a management exercise. *Harvard business review on decision making* (pp. 113-142). Cambridge, MA: Harvard Business School Press.

The situation could have improved if BP acknowledged that it did not know the true magnitude of the problem, but was actively working on it while trying various corrective actions. Although this transparent approach would not help contain the oil spill any sooner, it would foster better public perception, which is one of the major problems resulting from the spill. There is no doubt that BP did a suboptimal job communicating to the public, media, and stakeholders. Imagine being an employee during this time. Sadly, in cases like this, the media and other stakeholders take precedent. But in researching this crisis, the evidence points to the fact that internal communications were at the core of the cause of the disaster.

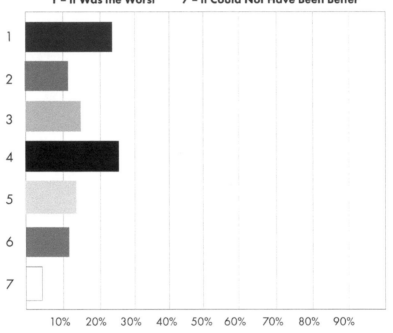

Respondents Assessment of Communication Leading Up To Change Initiative
1 = It Was the Worst   7 = It Could Not Have Been Better

Figure 7: RESPONDENTS' ASSESSMENT
OF COMMUNICATION

5 Predictor 2: Initial Change Reaction

When asked about their initial reaction when notified of the change initiative, only 2% of respondents had the most positive initial reaction that led them to believe that they would be promoted. The majority of respondents hovered between thinking they were going to lose their job to having no idea what it meant.[34] I know what you're thinking. It is like someone coming into the room and saying, "We have to talk." Of course, a good percentage of people will jump to an initial reaction that smacks of negativity. But as in most situations, much of any immediate cynicism can be attributed to the environment in which information is presented and discussed.

There are a couple of different ways to look at this. If the corporate climate is one in which there is little communication with executive leadership, and all of the sudden a memo goes out for a mandatory meeting where they will make an announcement, it is likely rumors will simmer and anxiety will prevail. The simple mention of an announcement may result in a doomsday theory in the eyes of some employees, as they see it as change they have no say in. This situation could be likened to the beginning of a workplace movie or novel drama, and would be the perfect point where our lead character gets shown the door.

---

[34] Data collected in Otis Johnson's Dissertation, Walden University February (2016). Where on a scale of 1= I am going to lose my job, and 7= I am going to get promoted

How do you alleviate employees jumping to that conclusion? The obvious answer is by making meetings with executive leadership a little more commonplace, by holding them when good things happen—as well as bad—including gatherings to celebrate the small things. The less obvious answer is if corporate leaders regularly engage employees on ways to improve the day-to-day productivity and work environment, when the meetings are called, employees will be less likely to jump to the conclusion of "bad news," because they've had an open door policy with management all along on how to optimize operations.

Respondents Initial Reaction When First Learning of Change Initiative
1 = I am going to lose my job   7 = I am going to get promoted

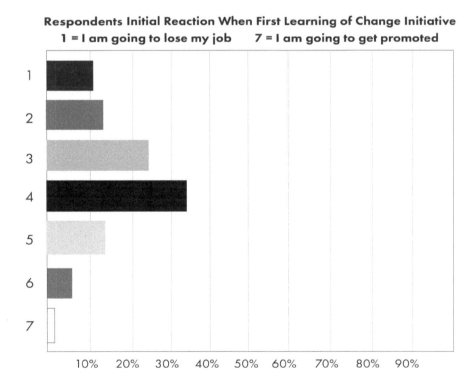

Figure 8: RESPONDENTS INITIAL REACTION WHEN FIRST LEARNING OF CHANGE INITIATIVE

The two primary dependent variables in this research were reaction to change (which includes the full spectrum of reactions ranging from active resistance to championing change) and support of change, which is further explored in three separate measures: compliance with change, cooperation with change, and championing of change—all of which we will explore later.

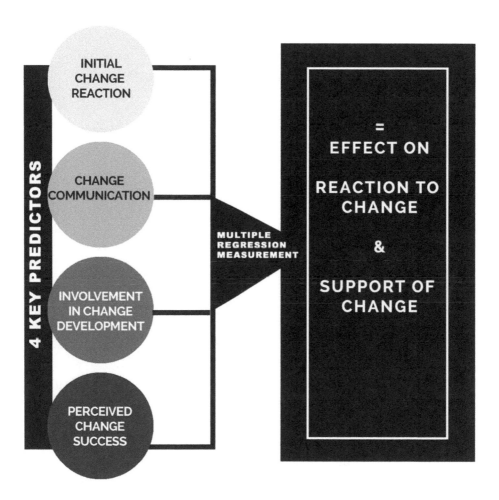

Figure 9: 4 KEY PREDICTOR EFFECT
ON REACTION AND SUPPORT

Remember my own story in which I was enthusiastic from the moment it was announced that change was coming—only to be blindsided by a policy that would prohibit me from taking on a leadership role in it? Had I been an employee in an environment which did not embrace input from all levels, I would most likely have been disgruntled. I would have probably thought that my department was being consolidated with others. Or, at the very least, I would have been ambivalent about the announcement. Instead, I was able to pick myself up and have the conversation that resulted in a change to the prohibitive policy, which in turn enabled me to not only champion the change once again, but make a significant contribution toward its ultimate success.

Team Reaction vs. Individual Reaction

In a large organization, teams create their own environments (for good or bad). For instance, even though my team successfully navigated the change implementation to come out in a better place, not all teams in my company did. Sometimes that's unavoidable, especially if the change initiative involves consolidating teams. But what is valuable is fostering a sense of ownership for teams so the environment they create within their subculture of the organization is supportive, and not defensive or cynical when faced with change.

Many management conferences and retreats bring in experts to help teams build trust and camaraderie while they work out ways to improve workflow processes while away from the office. Activities like these are valuable because they send a positive message up and down the ladder while being simple to grasp and enjoyable to participate in.

Imagine, if you will, a large conference room with about a dozen tables that seat about ten people each. The event organizer explains the rules to "15 things," an exercise where you, as an individual, have to rank a list of items at your disposal that you have to choose from to survive. There's a NASA version and a U.S. Coast Guard version. The NASA version has you stranded on the moon, some distance from where you were supposed to rendezvous, and the Coast Guard version has you taking these items in a life raft, not knowing how long it will be until help arrives. For simplicity's sake, let's use the life raft scenario.

You rank the fifteen things you chose from a supplied list in order of importance to you. Your list is then compared with the Coast Guard's official ranking.

The organizer collects the individual answers and then tells you to work with everyone at your table of 12 to agree upon the ranking of the same list; but as a team, you come up with only one list. Again, your team's answers are compared to the official rankings of the Coast Guard.

Which scores do you think consistently came out higher (meaning closest to the Coast Guard's)? According to one organizer, the team scores are not just consistently higher, they are *always* higher than the individual scores. The only time in this organizer's experience that an individual's rankings beat the team's rankings was when that individual was a Navy Seal.

If you take anything away from this book, let it be this: The combined contribution of the team is always greater than the team members' individual contributions. This is a valuable lesson at any rung of any business, especially for those at the top of the totem pole.

There's no doubt that, if faced with an actual life or death situation, there are some people you wish weren't sitting at your table. The funny thing is that these are the people who make us step out of our comfort zone and create meaningful change.

It is challenging to bring anything practical back to incorporate into the workplace after management retreats. On the surface, "15 things" is no different. If we were to go to the workplace and have individuals, teams and executive staff come up with their list of what is needed for the company to survive and stay competitive, chances are that when change comes around, the participants will have a more pro-active and positive initial change reaction. This type of inclusive leadership approach is characteristic of transformational leadership, which is designed to inspire individuals to actively participate in supporting, and creating, their new reality.

Transformational leadership has been the subject of many studies. Some define it as raising one another to higher levels of morality and motivation, or a process through which leaders inspire and motivate people based on collective purposes. Transformational leadership involves encouraging, facilitating, and accepting subordinate interests and input relating to organizational concerns and decision-making processes.[35] Transformational leadership is the type required to facilitate individual adaptive performance, as well as a climate of organizational innovation through teamwork. But it is important to realize that this type of leadership may work at both individual and team levels.

In short, transformational leadership is best suited to effectively lead change and, in general, if employees are motivated by transformational leaders, they will be more open and accepting to the news of impending change implementation resulting in a positive initial reaction. Transformational leadership fosters the feeling of "a good place to work." It leaves less of a reason for employees to bring fear into the equation as an initial reaction.

Fear is more likely to come into play at an individual level than as a team. But beware, because fear (and cynicism) can be contagious. Fear is more common individually because, as we know, everyone is different and anyone could be going through personal or professional challenges at any given moment—regardless of whether the change has been initiated or not.

Locus of control refers to a person's perception of their ability to exercise control over contextual elements of a situation, and individuals are referred to as being either internals or externals. Those who consider themselves internal believe they have control over their situations (i.e., that the locus of control is within them), and those who consider themselves external believe that situational factors control their lives (i.e., that the locus of control resides outside of them).

---

[35] Wang P., & Rode, J. C. (2010). Transformational leadership and follower creativity: The moderating effects of identification with leaders and organizational climate. Human Relations, 63(8), 1,105–1,128. http://dx.doi.org/10.1177/0018726709354132

Researchers concluded that internals would commit to change out of personal desire (affective) or obligation (normative), while externals would commit to change because of their perception of the costs associated with failure to support change (continuance). This is an important analysis for understanding the psychological mechanisms through which individuals with different loci of control react to change.[36]

As with most things, our initial change reaction can—and often does—change as more information is revealed. In my research, initial change reaction was one of the four key predictors of reaction to change, an all-encompassing factor that holds weight throughout the entire process of change implementation, from initial reaction through to the initiative's success or failure.

This variable of the way in which an employee reacts to large-scale organizational change fell on a continuum, ranging from a negative reaction of active resistance to a positive reaction of championing change. None of the four key predictors individually predicted the overall reaction to change or support of change. Of the four independent variables, initial change reaction was the only one that trended toward predicting the reaction to change, but the association was not significant. Together, the four factors predicted the reaction to change and the association was statistically significant. So, much like our individual approaches to "15 things for survival," the multidimensional input of the group as a whole, provides the results to better predict a successful outcome.

Much of the speed of transition will depend on the individual's self-perception, the locus of control, and other past experiences—and how these all combine to create their anticipation of future events. The more positive you see the outcome, the more control you have (or believe you have) over both the process and the final result, and the less difficult and negative a journey you have.

[36] Chen, J., & Wang, L. (2007). Locus of control and the three components of commitment to change. Personality and Individual Differences, 42(3), 503–512. doi:10.1016/j.paid.2006.07.025

6 Predictor 3: Involvement in Change Development

When successfully executed, large-scale change initiatives can reinforce an employee's commitment to their work and organization. I approached employee involvement in change as a multidimensional construct which, at its core, focuses on the emotional dimensions of employee commitment to change. To reiterate, involvement in change design is the degree to which an employee takes part in the planning and implementation of change.

Employees may be heavily involved in change design to the degree that they willingly cooperate, or even champion the proposed change as it is implemented. Alternatively, employees may be minimally involved or not involved at all. In my research, over 64% responded that they were not involved in the development of the change initiative, despite the fact that all participants in the survey were part of a change initiative. Just over 9% were actively involved, with the remaining respondents saying they were merely consulted (26%).

Much in the way transformational leadership theory has a majority of influence over initial change reaction, stakeholder theory has a major influence over how much employees or other stakeholders are involved in the change implementation. To be fair, recognizing that employees are important stakeholders is considered a technique of transformational leaders. However, the practice of stakeholder theory looks at ways to make this more of a working reality.

HOW INVOLVED RESPONDENTS WERE IN THE CHANGE INITIATIVE

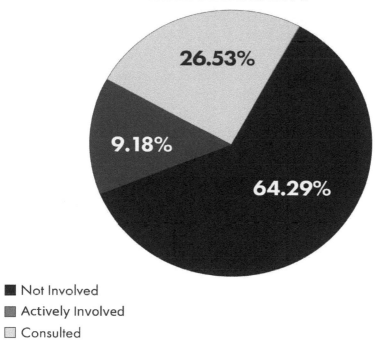

- ■ Not Involved
- ■ Actively Involved
- ☐ Consulted

Figure 10: RESPONDENTS' INVOLVEMENT

Stakeholder theory is about justice, acknowledgment, and fair treatment of those with a vested interest or stake in an organization.[37] Stakeholders are defined as key players, or those with stakes in an enterprise such as employees, owners, financiers, customers, communities, competitors, and government. This theory was developed for use in establishing equity in value creation, trade, ethics, capitalism, and management's role in dealing with those issues. As we've discussed, a lot of change stems from an organization's need to stay competitive, and positively affect the bottom line while also adhering

---

[37] Freeman, R. (1984). Strategic management: A stakeholder approach. Boston, MA: Pittman.

to regulatory demands. And as a result, the employees may be the last in this line of stakeholders that are considered when planning for organizational change. This low prioritization of employee interest is a mistake. Decisions and actions regarding change intimately and directly affect employees. For this reason, it makes perfect sense to say employees are important stakeholders to engage in the organizational change process. In case you forgot, 64% of respondents in my study said they had no involvement in change development.

To recap, 50–80% of one of the most prevalent forms of large-scale change (mergers and acquisitions) fail. And given the vast number and types of other corporate change initiatives, it is difficult to accurately determine how many of the other types of change implementation succeed or fail. What we do know is that the level of employee involvement in the change implementation plays a pivotal role in success rates. Given that the percentage of respondents who did not have involvement in change development falls directly in the midst of the one type of large-scale change which has a measurable success rate, one may be able to presume the data corresponds to other types of change implementation.

It is not a stretch to conclude that employees' participation in change development is a key factor to successful organizational change implementation.[38]

A balanced, stakeholder-oriented approach to organizational change should address the views, concerns, needs, and efforts of various stakeholders—especially those of employees when considering and managing change. An integrated approach that considers employees as important stakeholders to engage in organizational change necessary for change success, should also include a balanced approach that considers all of the variables of initial change reaction,

---

[38] Jaros, S. (2010). Commitment to organizational change: A critical review. Journal of Change Management, 10(1), 79–108. doi:10.1080/14697010903549457

Whelan-Berry, K., & Somerville, K. (2010). Linking change drivers and the organizational change process: A review and synthesis. Journal of Change Management, 10(2), 175–193. doi:10.1080/14697011003795651

involvement in change design, perceived change success, and change communication—individually and in aggregate.

Additionally, my results related to the championing of change subscale, suggest a connection between seeing employees as stakeholders and employees championing change. Simply put, employees are supportive and enthusiastic when they are involved, feel instrumental to an organization's overall success, and when leaders treat them as stakeholders.[39] My results on the championing change subscale suggest that transformational leadership during change might include ensuring that employees are made to feel like stakeholders with an interest in the organization. In addition, stakeholder theory may offer a way to better understand that successful change should include a balanced approach that considers a variety of strategies when it comes to employee concerns, and may have a specific connection to employees championing change by involving them, and making them feel crucial to an organization's success.

In addition to a thorough communication plan, change agents ensure that employees at all levels of the organization are involved in the change. Change agents can do so through soliciting feedback in informal settings, and delivering the feedback to management for action and communication back to employees. When contemplating organizational change, managers should create a targeted change management strategy that, at a minimum, includes a contingent of change agents to facilitate informal employee engagement, a stakeholder information needs analysis for timely and relevant dissemination of information, and a process realization office responsible for communication quality, frequency, and consistency.

Take, for instance, when change management was introduced at a traditional print-based, global, publishing company fully preparing to embrace digital-age publishing, and to implement changes relating to online publication and delivery systems. Researchers found that preparing employees for the change through hands-on inclusion techniques caused them to support change implementation and increased the change success. The inclusive, hands-on tech-

---

[39] 2014 Eskreis-winkler, Duckworth, Shulman and Beal.

niques examined included workshops on leading, implementing, and experiencing the dynamics and expectations of change, as well as pre- and post-event webinars with follow-up activities.[40] As we consider these inclusion techniques, it is easy to see how change communication not only feeds employee involvement in change design, but also opens the door for valuable insights that change leaders may not have considered—simply because they have a different point of view of day-to-day operations.

In my research, I came across a contradiction that seems to have a simple solution. Researchers found that adequate change planning is crucial for successful change, and at the same time, many change efforts fail from lack of adequate resources and planning.[41] I couldn't help but think that if resources were a problem, it is all the more reason to involve employees in the change development process. Think about the old saying, "If you want something done right, do it yourself." If you want your employees (and company) to successfully navigate the uncertainty of major change, let them in on the process design. Here is a good place for my occasional reminder that people don't hate change, they hate not having a say in it.

Some researchers in the field recommend that human resources departments take a strategic approach to change that facilitates it by supporting teamwork, as organizations work through change. This approach should emphasize relational leadership capabilities in human resource managers in addition to technical skills.[42] Like others, the findings of this study suggest that employee involvement in the change process through teamwork was a key success factor of change management. Furthermore, the study had valuable, practical infor-

---

[40] Franckeiss, A. (2012). Organizational and individual change: A case study. Strategic HR Review, 11(5), 278–282. http://dx.doi.org/10.1108/14754391211248693

[41] Whelan-Berry, K., & Somerville, K. (2010). Linking change drivers and the organizational change process: A review and synthesis. Journal of Change Management, 10(2), 175–193. doi:10.1080/14697011003795651

[42] Barratt-Pugh, L., Bahn, S., & Gakere, E. (2013). Managers as change agents: Implications for human resource managers engaging with culture change. Journal of Organizational Change Management, 26(4), 748–764. doi:10.1108/JOCM-Feb-2011-0014

mation on the kinds of informal relational skills needed by human resource managers to manage effective organizational change.[43]

Large-scale change initiatives, if executed well, can reinforce an employee's commitment to their work and organization. Therefore, unless change leaders are out to sabotage the outcome of the change initiative, there really is no reason not to involve employees in the development of the change initiative.

In short, firms need stakeholders to exist. It has been argued, that seeing employees as stakeholders can help organizations increase social responsibility and achieve performance improvement.[44] As stakeholders, employees are greatly important to an organization's sense of social responsibility, because organizational decisions and actions—including decisions and actions regarding change—intimately affect them. Furthermore, stakeholder engagement and identification are keys to social responsibility because of issues concerning compensation, employment security, and skill development. So, seeing employees as integral to a firm's existence, as stakeholders, may reinforce employees' participation in change endeavors, which has been found to be a key factor to successful organizational change implementation.[45] In other words, employees may have an interest in organizational change not only as employees (how the change will affect their day-to-day operations) but also as stakeholders (the overall effect of change on the organization's success and well-being).

Researchers have also used stakeholder theory to examine organizational change based on the need for organizations to transition to more sustainable paradigms. The struggles of moving from a techno-centric change management paradigm, focused on business behav-

---

[43] Goksoy, A., Ozsoy, B., & Vayvay, O. (2012). Business process reengineering: Strategic tool for managing organizational change an application in a multinational company. International Journal of Business and Management, 7(2), 89–112. doi:10.5539/ijbm.v7n2p89

[44] Parmar, B., Freeman, R. E., Harrison, J., Wicks, A., de Colle, S., & Purnell, L. (2010). Stakeholder theory: The state of the art. Cambridge, UK: Cambridge University Press.

[45] Jaros, S. (2010). Commitment to organizational change: A critical review. Journal of Change Management, 10(1), 79–108. doi:10.1080/14697010903549457

ior, to one that is more inclusive, and considers multiple stakeholders associated with individual businesses, is a good example. Why, after 14 years of advocacy from management researchers for a paradigm shift, has the field of change management not been able to shift from a techno-centric paradigm? What is required to move toward an alternative paradigm? Finally, after employing critical systems theory to develop a 3-phased process model—one that advocated a more comprehensive approach, which considered the interconnectedness of social and economic factors, as well as associated stakeholders of a particular business targeted for change—the paradigm shift had some momentum. The implications of this framework are twofold. First, it addresses the interconnectedness of social, economic, organizational, and ecological issues. Second, it recognizes the effects that multiple and diverse agents with little authority can have on change. Although the model does not focus on employees, by now you know considering employees as an important part of the interconnected network of agents that influence change processes can be the difference between success and failure.[46]

Others have approached the study of stakeholder theory from the perspectives of social capital, sustainability, and trust. For example, the differences in approach to corporate social responsibility, and treatment of stakeholders based on the size of the organization (large or small to mid-sized), found that larger organizations focused more on stakeholder theory, while small to mid-sized organizations focused on building social capital. Corporate social responsibility has evolved into a service objective of organizations with a genuine interest in doing good for the communities in which they operate; which, in turn, has positive implications, not only for the company's reputation, but for the employees feeling good about what they dedicate a vast majority of their daily efforts toward.[47]

---

[46] Valente, M. (2010). Demystifying the struggles of private sector paradigmatic change: Business as an agent in a complex adaptive system. Business & Society, 49, 439–476. doi:10.1177/0007650310369376

[47] Russo, A., & Perrini, F. (2009). Investigating stakeholder theory and social capital: CSR in large firms and SMEs. Journal of Business Ethics, 91(2), 207–221. doi:10.1007/s10551-009-0079-z

In related research, a model that helps understand stakeholder management—from both an organizational and globally environmental perspective—shifted focus from simply ensuring the organization's product is the best it could be for customers to ensuring a good working environment for employees as well.[48] They expanded the stakeholder management concept to include not only employees' concerns, but to limiting damage to the environment in which the organization operates as a way to create sustainability. It has been argued that organizations have an ethical obligation to treat their stakeholders fairly, but that less powerful stakeholders are at risk of unfair treatment. Here is a good place to recall that low man on the totem pole holding up all of those that are higher.

Sustainable organizational change requires a balanced approach that acknowledges stakeholder needs. Change that focuses exclusively on the traditional bottom line of reducing cycle time and operating cost—while increasing productivity and revenue for the business at the expense of stakeholder concerns and social responsibility—most likely won't facilitate an organization's sustainable future. Organizations, therefore, must consider influences beyond the immediate business needs of the organization, and commit to a shift toward more responsible business practices that balance economic drivers with social and environmental objectives. This shift is necessary for sustainable change implementation as organizations focus on the system as a whole, and not just the manifestations of the underlying business struggles. Most recent studies indicate that such a shift has begun. But without consideration of the multiple stakeholders and relationships typical of a complex system, this shift to more socially-conscious change management is not likely to continue.

In my experience, had I not been involved in the change development (if my change leader did not recognize the absurdity of needing the word *manager* in my title, to enable me to continue my

[48] Garvare, R., & Johansson, P. (2010). Management for sustainability – A stakeholder theory. Total Quality Management & Business Excellence, 21(7), 737–744. doi:10.1080/14783363.2010.483095

efforts), much of the foundational change that I had already been championing would have gone away. Aside from my loss of work and pride, my entire team would have been in a different place when it came to the change implementation, the ramifications of not having proper clinical trial management oversight (not to mention the negative bottom line results) would have all had multidimensional effect on failure—instead of the success we realized.

Small Changes Can Support Success of Major Initiatives.

When I first joined the clinical research operations group, I was assigned a clinical research study that was in jeopardy of missing an important milestone (achieving the last patient enrolled). This was an especially challenging project because the team had already implemented a robust patient enrollment advertising strategy.

I conducted a quick lessons learned analysis to get to the root cause of the patient enrollment problem. One of the most important findings was that the screener, used to interview patients responding to the advertising campaign, did not address the most common reasons why patients were not meeting study eligibility requirements. Once those three additional questions were added, study enrollment completed within a few weeks, eliminating the need to extend timelines.

Employees in the trenches can often offer invaluable input that would have never been thought of by a change agent or even a transformational leader. People don't hate change, they hate not having a say in it and, unfortunately, all too often this lack of involvement leads to an unsuccessful implementation of change.

7 Predictor 4: Perceived Change Success

Regardless of how much employees are considered stakeholders, inspired to champion change by transformational leadership, or are involved in the development of change initiatives, they will rarely be privy to the bottom-line numbers that will likely determine if the change can be considered successful. And that's okay. Perceived change success refers to the degree to which employees perceive the proposed change to be completely and effectively implemented. Perception is a funny thing.

Aside from benefits and pay, some of the factors that can impact employee perception include how well the employer communicates with employees, the nature of the working conditions, the policies and procedures of the business in general, and how much trust and respect is present between managers, employees, and coworkers. Clearly, during a large-scale change initiative, *all* of these things are tenuous at best. Is it possible that employee perception of whether a change was successful or not is decided long before the implementation is complete? Unless the change being implemented is at a core level that overhauls current procedures, chances are the answer is yes.

A lot of the perception has to do with where the employee is on the career ladder. Some employees may not be there for a career, but for a job, to get them by until what they really want to do can be realized. However, the perception of success can directly influence the outcome of any large-scale initiative to far-reaching effect long after the employee has moved on. In any case, you can sway this perception—both during and after the change has occurred—to be a positive reality.

In my research, perceived change success was a variable measured by a single survey question for which employees chose their agreement on a scale of 1-7, where 1 = "A complete failure," and 7 = "A resounding success." Only 6% claimed the large-scale change they were involved in was, "A resounding success." Given the fact that more than 75% of respondents were involved in change that wasn't due to downsizing (or upsizing), or other initiatives that tend to generate cynicism, one would think that it was in their best interest to see the change succeed. Looking at it from another angle, more than 75% of respondents were involved in change that centered on mergers, acquisition, process redesign or internal restructuring, to ostensibly better the company—yet, only 6% perceived the change as a resounding success.

Now, considering what we've learned about how much previous change attempts affect new change initiatives, this percentage should be even more disturbing. When it comes to implementation of a successful, large-scale change, there are no do-overs.

To be fair, only slightly over 10% deemed the process they were involved in was, "A complete failure." Still, when so much is at stake, 10% is pretty high, and if the employee base feels it was a failure, it's pretty safe to say that low-man is supporting the same conclusion that is on a spreadsheet coveted by the man atop the totem pole.

As you can see in the chart below (*Figure 11*), with majority of respondents in the middle, it is clear that a lot of respondents were on the fence in determining their perception of success. But when so much is at stake, financially and socially, hitting the average isn't something to celebrate when you need to be above average to stay competitive, and way above average to make a difference in the status quo.

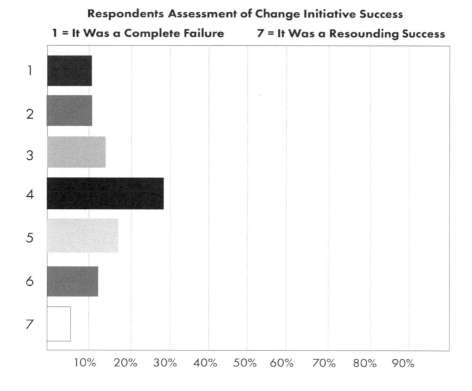

Figure 11: RESPONDENTS' ASSESSMENT OF SUCCESS

Let's use, for example, a merger or acquisition scenario. Remember, this is one type of large-scale change where we have concrete success and failure numbers. In a typical new employee onboarding session, there is some sort of time spent with the human resources department that includes a review of the company's policies and procedures. Now, imagine two corporate cultures merging, and a seasoned employee of one of the entities now has to become familiar with the other company's policies and procedures manual—just as if they were a new hire again. That's probably the biggest blind date on record. This new reality affects their standing as an experienced employee within the organization and, more importantly, their security. Even if only at a subconscious level, the residual of the effect remains.

Suffice it to say, large-scale change needs good coordination, as it typically affects multiple departments and requires a coordinated whole system approach.[49] This whole system approach entails examining the change from multiple angles. First, change managers (including human resource managers) must consider the actual entity requiring change, along with the associated objectives. Next, change managers must consider the process of getting from the current state to the desired state. Finally, change agents must understand the provisions to put in place to support these two previous components of organizational change. All of this requires a whole system approach that may obligate significant change to an organization's governance policy—which incidentally brings us back to the idea of including employees in the development of the change initiative. Think about it, if you have to create a new policy and procedure (especially as it relates to production), wouldn't the employees who have to carry it out be more likely to embrace it if they had a say in designing or developing it?

In my research, perceived change success was the closest variable to being an independent significant predictor of championing change. Though this association was not statistically significant, directionally, perceptions of the change's success influence the degree to which employees support the change. Recall that championing change is the most enthusiastic support of change, followed by cooperation, then compliance. By now, I hope you can see the relationship of these variables to each other.

---

[49] Radwan, S. (2010). Taking a whole system approach to adopting policy governance. Board Leadership, 108, 6–8. http://boardleadershipnewsletter.com

Part 3

What's at Stake?

Change of the magnitude of an organizational restructure, whether due to mergers and acquisitions or other drivers, has the potential to disrupt a company's performance, success, and growth if not handled effectively and efficiently.

8 Trading the Old for the New

We're hopelessly lost, but making good time.
—Yogi Berra

The effect of the four key predictors (initial change reaction, change communication, involvement in change development, and perceived change success) on the two dependent variables was the basis for my research. The two dependent variables were the reaction to change and support of change.

Reaction to change includes the full spectrum of reactions ranging from active resistance to championing change. Specifically:

- *Active Resistance.* Demonstrating opposition in response to change by engaging in overt behaviors that are intended to ensure the change fails.
- *Passive Resistance.* Demonstrating opposition in response to change by engaging in covert or subtle behaviors aimed at preventing the success of change.
- *Compliance.* Demonstrating minimum support for a change by going along with the change, but doing so reluctantly.
- *Cooperation.* Demonstrating support for a change by exerting effort when it comes to the change, going along with the spirit of the change, and being willing to make small sacrifices.

- *Championing.* Demonstrating extreme enthusiasm for a change by going above and beyond what is formally required to ensure the success of the change.

When participants in my study were asked which best represented their reaction to change, almost 43% responded with compliance, with over 14% falling in the negative space of this scale, by either actively resisting or passively resisting. Is it any surprise that this total of 57% correlates with the lower end of the 50-80% of failed mergers and acquisitions?

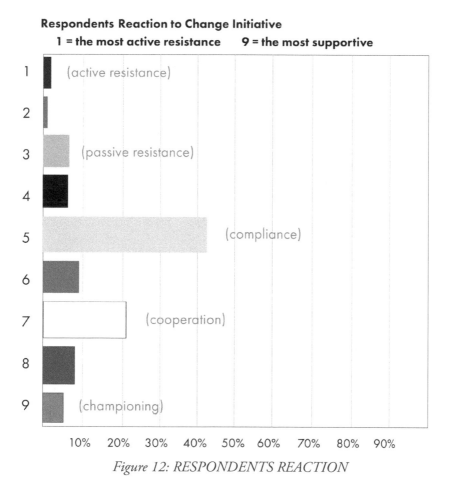

Figure 12: RESPONDENTS REACTION

Support of change was also expressed as three separate measures: compliance, cooperation, and championing, and I calculated a composite index of support of change, as the mean of the three subscales (*compliance, cooperation,* and *championing*).

In summary, the four independent variables (initial change reaction, change communication, involvement in change development, and perceived change success), in aggregate, significantly predicted the overall reaction to change. And though they did not significantly predict support of change overall, they did predict the championing subscale of support of change with statistical significance.

A huge factor in predicting reaction, and the subsequent success of a change implementation, is for employees, as stakeholders at all levels, to understand not only the "new model," but to understand what happens to the old model. Here, we look at the way change is introduced by identifying what is going to stay the same, what is going away and what is going to be new and why it should be better for each level of employee in the organization. How does what all stakeholders need for success affect everyone else? Remember, to employees, change in productivity, responsibility or quality of work environment are the pain triggers discussed in Chapter 2. The psychology of change management theory's social and organizational model is driven by the process in which organizations move from a position of stasis into a new position or perspective. This new perspective can be broken down into three stages of change: the unfreezing (the undoing of an established mindset or approach), the actual change (which involves a certain degree of uncertainty about the future), and freezing (the establishment of a new mindset or position).

In response to large-scale organizational change associated with corporate mergers, evolving business environments, and increasingly globalized markets, studies began to emerge on how to manage adaptive and organizational change, some of which used change management theory as the theoretical framework.[50] In one example

---

[50] Ruta, C. (2005). The application of change management theory to HR portal implementation in subsidiaries of multinational corporations. Human Resource Management, 44(1), 35-53. doi:10.1002/hrm.20039

of change management theory, as it relates to process communication, researchers explored how transformational leadership could be used to guide and manage change at a South Carolina hospital. The researchers used a qualitative research design to gain insight from a sample of nurses during a Magnet recognition program which ran for three years. Magnet recognition was a credentialing status designed to attract, recruit, and retain quality nurses.

Thirty-five nurses participated in focus groups. Of the thirty-five nurses, six were managers, thirty-four were female, and one was male. Over half of the participants achieved at least a Bachelor of Science in Nursing degree, and the median experience of the group was twenty years. The researchers based their theoretical framework on Kotter's change model[51] and the attributes of transformational leadership. Three major themes concerning the perceived change of the hospital emerged: recognition, resources, and culture.

All participants were aware of the prestigious value of the Magnet award, and they all identified recognition as the primary result of it. However, nurse managers and staff disagreed on resources. Managers thought the hospital had become a more attractive place to work resulting in fewer overtime expenses, while staff thought the Magnet recognition had little or no effect on resources. Changes in culture were less noticeable as staff expected something radical to happen that did not happen—while nurse managers saw incremental change associated with research, retention, and increased overall quality.

Although the study provided valuable information on how employees of differing levels perceive change and its consequences, a key limitation of this study was other important stakeholders, such as patients, physicians, and family members, were not included in the sample. These stakeholders could have provided useful insight about their experiences and perceptions of change. Additionally, a pre-Magnet survey would have also served as a good baseline comparison. But the one thing that stands out to me is the fact that the staff expected something radical to happen that did not.

---

[51] Kotter, J. (1996). Leading change. Harvard Business Press.

If employees at one level perceive the results to look a certain way, while their managers perceive the results to be something else, there is a major disconnect in communicating the nature of the change and the goal that will be measured to determine its success. I'm sure you can see the interconnectedness and importance of clearly aligning the three stages to arrive at the new perspective that organizational change is about.

Much like my multi-dimensional construct of determining reaction to change, researchers also developed a multi-dimensional construct to study commitment to change based on three dimensions: affective (positive feelings toward commitment), normative (perceived obligation to comply), and continuance (perceived consequences of failure to comply).[52]

Three studies tested a three-component model of workplace commitment to change. Study number one consisted of 224 graduate psychology students, studies two and three involved hospital nurses from various medical facilities. For these two studies, the researchers hypothesized that employees experience three commitment-to-change mindsets (affective commitment to change, normative commitment to change, and continuance commitment to change) that could predict change-oriented behavior better than organizational commitment could.

The researchers found that when seen as a behavioral continuum of change-support actions, commitment to change was a better predictor of behavioral support for change than was organizational commitment. More specifically, affective commitment to change positively predicted support in both samples, while normative commitment to change positively predicted support in one sample and not the other. However, continuance commitment to change did not predict change support in either sample. At its most basic level, the results indicate that we cannot comfortably support a level of change without a clear end in sight, and forcing change through punishment

[52] Herscovitch, L., & Meyer, J. (2002). Commitment to organizational change: Extension of a three-component model. Journal of Applied Psychology, 87(3), 474–487. doi:10.1037//0021-9010.87.3.474

and consequences is not an effective way to implement meaningful, sustainable change.

Another set of researchers studied individuals' commitment to the change itself as well as their organizational commitment in thirty-four different public and private organizations. Data from 806 managers and office workers surmised that both kinds of commitment were best approached as a three-way interaction between an individual's favorableness to the change, the extent of change, and the impact of change on the individual's job.[53] They found that considering change at multiple levels was necessary to gain a better understanding of individual employees' reactions to change, and concluded that assessments of change at different organizational levels may help to explain individual-level responses to change.

Getting employees to commit to new procedures, policies, and goals involving change increased the likelihood of change success. The commitment to the new operating norms may be hard to achieve without a comprehensive, multidimensional approach to change management.[54] One finding remains clear: communication regarding organizational change is important for employee adoption and support of change.

There is no "one-size-fits-all" approach to organizational change. The results of my study suggest that factors connected to the unfreezing of established approaches (i.e., reaction to change and support of change), could not be predicted by initial change reaction, involvement in change design, perceived change success, and change communication, individually. Consequently, the results do not support targeting any of these components individually to help successfully unfreeze established practices in facilitating successful change. After all, an organization cannot truly unfreeze its operations

---

[53] Fedor, D., Caldwell, S., & Herold, D. (2006). The effects of organizational changes on employee commitment: A multivariate analysis. Personnel Psychology, 59(1), 1–29. http://dx.doi.org/10.1111/j.1744-6570.2006.00852.x.

[54] Fedor, D., Caldwell, S., & Herold, D. (2006). The effects of organizational changes on employee commitment: A multivariate analysis. Personnel Psychology, 59(1), 1–29. http://dx.doi.org/10.1111/j.1744-6570.2006.00852.x

to implement change. It must continue to operate the full business and deliver results during the change. It is like flying an airplane while building it, which is why the quality and frequency of change communication is so important. However, initial change reaction, involvement in change design, perceived change success, and change communication may be used—in aggregate—to generate information that could be used to help unfreeze established practices in relation to reaction to change, and the championing subscale of support of change.

A well-coordinated process might also ensure that key players are aware of the decisions and the role they need to play to support it. This process is policy deployment, the second of a four-step approach to organizational strategy. The other steps are policy setting, implementation, and review. If you've been paying attention until now, you know these four steps will ideally involve the employee being a part of their development. This process begins with an identified solution and focuses on achieving the intended goals of that solution.[55]

In addition to communication and employee involvement, good process management is essential to successful change implementation. In a large-scale organizational change situation, such as a merger or acquisition, the organizations should consider using various process management tools to foster communication—up, down, and across the organization. First, the organizations should establish a process realization office. This office would be responsible for coordinating all formal integration-related communication, including town hall meetings to present high-level integration strategies. This central office could serve as a trusted source of merger- or integration-related information, create consistency in messaging, and represent a communication brand for the change initiative. With such an organized process, employees would know where to go for reliable organizational change information.

---

[55] Watson, G. H. (2005). Design and execution of a collaborative business strategy. Journal for Quality and Participation, 28(4), 4–10. http://asq.org/pub/jqp/

9 Managing Up

The strength of the lowest man on the totem
pole determines how high it reaches.

Perhaps you're familiar with the Dr. Seuss story entitled *Yertle the Turtle*. Here is a refresher. Yertle was the king of the pond and, as such, he ruled all that he saw. One day, he got the idea that he needed to see more. In order to do this, he knew he must get to a higher vantage point than the pond level. So, he called up nine underlings from the pond, stacked them all up and climbed on top. He was thrilled with the new things he could see and the things he now ruled as a result.

But the turtle at the very bottom, of the stack, a turtle named Mac, complained that this new vantage point was breaking his back. Yertle got annoyed and called for 900 more turtles to gain an even better height advantage. Yertle was drunk with power, and Mac wished he was drunk to numb his misery. Mac made his famous statement, "I know up on top you are seeing great sights, but down here on the bottom, we too should have rights."

Yertle again ignored him and called for 5,607 more turtles. Mac tried to complain but burped instead. The burp caused a chain reaction that toppled the stack of turtles. Yertle was now, forevermore, king of the mud.

Of course, this is a caricature drama to teach a lesson in greed and selfishness. However, it also perfectly depicts the organizational dilemma that can occur when the powers that be decide on large-scale change without considering the employee base that is holding them up.

Many change management experts will advise executive staff of the need to assign change agents to oversee change implementation. These change agents usually come from the ranks of middle management. If you recall, in my situation, the requisite for being a change agent was that I had to have the word *manager* in my title. On the surface, these approaches seem logical. However, there are situations—as in my case—in which these artificial or arbitrary restrictions can adversely affect the success of the change initiative.

Important considerations when assigning someone to oversee change implementation:

1) The change agent assigned to manage the process of change isn't necessarily the manager of the process that is changing, so they have no affinity to the team they are now helping navigate this challenging time.
2) The change agent assigned may not have the leadership experience to manage up. In this situation, they may be assigned because they are good at project management in general, or because they are part of the human resources team.
3) In their previously established roles, the change agent may not have a lot of interaction with executive staff. This results in them not having the experience, and in some cases, the courage, to present the consequences of a change implementation that was not thoroughly planned out.

Studies indicate that no matter how generous the benefits and how accommodating the workplace environment is, if an employee has an inefficient manager relationship, they are likely to give up those perks for a position which may have fewer benefits but a healthier manager/employee relationship.[56] When the plan for change is introduced, some employees react by looking for another job; not because of the new process they will be expected to take on, but because of the person managing the change process, which adds to that high cost of turnover we discussed.

Good managers come in many shapes and sizes, and great managers stand out by also being leaders. Leaders keep the big picture in mind and inspire their reports to follow them toward that goal. Whereas managers are more in the moment at hand, and know how to effectively facilitate that moment so that progress can be made to move on to the next phase. There are many management studies and business advice resources on how to be a better manager. Those are not the focus of this book. Rather, it is focused on considerations related to initiating and following through on change implementation, starting with initial change announcement.

Like employees, change agents are crucial to successful change implementation. Not only do they manage change processes, they also have to manage people and emotions, often with no authority other than their ability to influence. It is that simple, and that is hard.

Think of a teacher, or even a mentor who influenced you, who recognized your unique approach to learning and fostered your strengths so that you could get the most out of the knowledge they were trying to impart. Many of us have had at least one of these figures in our formative years, regardless of our social, economic or academic status. These influencers from our youth have the same qualities of influencers in our careers. They are great managers.

It is not easy to be a great manager. Managing others is one of the most difficult undertakings a human can face. Managers are jugglers of resources, tasks and personalities. In most organizations, resources are limited, tasks are numerous and personalities are individual and all over the spectrum of human emotions. So, great managers also have to be great observers and delegators. They have to be able to identify the talents of those in their charge and empower them to recognize their own potential.

---

56 The Gallup Organization, Compilation 1999

Tough love is often required during organizational change. You are not going to please everyone. It is impossible and goes against the grain of the disruption effective change requires. However, the percentage of employees who actively resist change can be lowered through better change management. By now, you know what I'm going to remind you of: people don't hate change, they hate not having a say in it.

Researchers recently noted that because of its ubiquity and inevitability, large-scale change represents potential organizational discontinuity and, consequently, effective change management has become a major component of organizational success—even when there is no active change in the process.[57] The pharmaceutical industry is especially subject to organizational discontinuity related to large-scale change. So, for me, examining studies on change management were appropriate for contextualizing and framing my study.

My study was designed to understand and document employee reactions that indicate their level of reaction to change and how it relates to their support of change. Researchers Herscovitch and Meyer identified three operationalized measures of support of change: compliance (minimum supportive behavior), cooperation (more supportive), and championing (the highest level of support).[58] These operationalized measures, along with active and passive resistance, encompass reaction to change and form the full spectrum of employee response to change examined in my study.

Whelan-Berry & Somerville isolated four key contributors to successful change:

(a) A clear vision of change
(b) Leaders' change-related actions

[57] Deeg, J. (2009). Organizational discontinuity: Integrating evolutionary and revolutionary change theories. Management Revue, 20(2), 190–208. doi:10.1688/1861-9908

[58] Herscovitch, L., & Meyer, J. (2002). Commitment to organizational change: Extension of a three-component model. Journal of Applied Psychology, 87(3), 474–487. doi:10.1037//0021-9010.87.3.474

(c) Change-related communication, training, and employee participation

(d) Aligned human resources practices and organizational structure and processes.

Their theory-building article contributed to my research literature by identifying major factors of change, and discussing how they relate to the change process in order to manage organizational change more effectively.

Based on a synthesis of the literature on change management, it appears that inclusion of employees in organizational change implementation increases their support of change.[59] And viewing employees as stakeholders concerned with an organization's overall success may help establish a bottoms-up approach to including employees in the change process, which also helps employees be more supportive and enthusiastic because they feel they are important to an organization's overall success. In addition, researchers found that employees can have a nuanced reaction to change, that they do not always outright support or resist change. In fact, employees can both resist and support aspects of the same change, and personal attitudes toward change interacts with their attitudes toward the change agent, which can result in ambivalence.[60] Additionally, effective change management also includes clear communication of change before and during implementation—as well as employee and organizational change histories as other key factors in successful organizational change.

Parallel to these initiatives, transformational leadership, an inclusive leadership style that includes the concerns and views of subordinates, has proven effective in organizational change because it can include employees in the planning and implementation of

---

[59] Barratt-Pugh et al., 2013; Budhwar et al., 2009; Franckeiss, 2012; Goksoy et al., 2012; Marks & Mirvis, 2011; Shibayama et al., 2011; Whelan-Berry & Sommerville, 2010

[60] Mishra & Bhatnagar, 2010; Oreg & Sverdlik, 2011

change.[61] It is also contended that transformational leadership is the type required for effective change management because transformational leaders use motivation and inspiration to help employees adapt to organizational change. Additionally, creating a work environment conducive to innovation fosters better change adoption at individual and team levels.

Based on the results of my study, it may be possible to construct a more effective change management process with an optimum mix of leadership and employee engagement. The effects of employee engagement during change can be optimized in an innovative, transformational leadership environment, where employees identify with leaders. The four key predictors of response to change in my study (initial change reaction, involvement in change design, perceived change success, and change communication) can assist, in the aggregate, in creating such an environment.

Communication and employee involvement are vital to the way employees react to organizational change. Therefore, managers contemplating change need to consider and decide from the outset what information to share with employees, communication frequency, and how much to engage employees in the process. This practice may be different from the traditional approach of focusing on the financial and regulatory aspects of the deal first; then worrying about change implementation and employee reaction later. The important thing to realize here is that the change agents are the fulcrum to the success. This means that just as they need to be transformational and inclusive leaders to the employees below them on the totem pole, they also need to be given the autonomy to manage up, by regularly communicating and including the upper tier of the totem pole in the change process—because the reality of large-scale change often needs to be fluid enough for modification along the way. Likewise, this same upper tier of executive management needs to adopt a transformational and inclusive style of great management toward these change agents in the field.

---

[61] Charbonnier-Voirin, El Akremi, & Vandenberghe, 2010; Ricke-Kiely & Robey-Williams, 2011; Wang & Rode, 2010

10 Where Do We Go from Here?

In my research, almost 41% of respondents said they received change-related communication less than once a month. This is astonishing. If we have learned anything about the synergy of these predictors of reactions that lead to success, it is that everything starts with communication.

Again, 50–80% of mergers and acquisitions fail because of clashing corporate cultures, a lack of clear communication, and a lack of employee involvement in the change. Clearly, every situation is different, but by stepping back and looking at these three areas alongside the four key predictors, every situation could have a much greater probability of successful implementation of large-scale change.

For example, product lifecycles in electronic companies may be short, but pharmaceutical companies must constantly focus on innovation because of the long development timeline needed to bring medicines and therapies to consumers. Therefore, pharmaceutical companies may need to adopt business process reengineering practices to improve operational processes so they can maximize patent life to recoup drug discovery and development expenses for profit. Also relevant to, and reflected in my study, is that the researchers found employee involvement in the change process through teamwork and change communication to be key success factors of change management.

For mergers and acquisitions, some research points to the need for further integrative study of the role of human resources departments in all three stages of the process: pre-integration, integration, and unification.[62] Because mergers and acquisitions occur on a global scale, study of cultural differences as they pertain to organizational operations and employees during change is increasingly important. The top priority in the mergers and acquisitions process is always getting the financial component of the deal right while adhering to applicable regulatory requirements.

In the pharmaceutical industry, the pipeline of products is next in the line of priorities, while "softer" cultural issues have ranked low on the priority list.[63] Consequently, the researchers promoting the integrative study created a framework that worked with culture as a core consideration in the mergers and acquisitions process. Given that a large percentage of these undertakings fail making the financial deal a moot point, this is the right approach.

The framework created is to assist human resources departments in managing issues associated with acculturation in the mergers and acquisitions process. For this framework, the researchers used change management theory and highlighted the value of organizations devising a clear "cultural end state." The four, distinct cultural end states include, (a) pluralism (partner companies co-exist), (b) integration (partners blend current cultures together), (c) assimilation (one company absorbs the other), and (d) transformation (partner companies merge key elements and adopt new norms and values). The framework and end state plan, point back to the simple suggested approach: "Here's what's going away, here's what's going to stay, here's what's going to be new, this is why we're doing it, and this is where you fit in."

---

[62] Budhwar, P., Varma, A., Katou, A., & Narayan, D. (2009). The role of HR in cross-border mergers and acquisitions: The case of Indian pharmaceutical firms. The Multinational Business Review, 17(2), 89–110. http://dx.doi.org/10.1108/1525383x200900011

[63] Marks, M., & Mirvis, P. (2011). A framework for the human resources role in managing culture in mergers and acquisitions. Human Resource Management, 50(6), 859–877. http://dx.doi.org/10.1002/hrm.20445

No matter how difficult change is, in any aspect of the human condition, if the initial communication can address these core pain triggers, the implementation of the change will flow much more smoothly.

Classic change management theory helps to frame the notion that human resources must unfreeze extant, cultural mindsets to move people toward the desired cultural end state, and then refreeze the newly desired culture. However, when it comes to mergers and acquisitions, a company should note early in the process which entity will take a dominant role in specific aspects of the merged organization. Such an approach to M&A-related change could fast track and could optimize the desired cultural end state, which is important to success.

Organizations do not need to, nor should they, wait until they are essentially forced to change. They should always be prepared for change by engaging in communication as a fluid process management approach. Organizations should have a change strategy that includes a contingent of change agents who are ready to facilitate change initiatives.[64] Some suggest that change provisions include both a communication plan and change agents. However, if the culture is one of welcome engagement, communication should already be a part of the day-to-day reality. This is your last reminder: people don't hate change; they hate not having a say in it. So, if open communication gives them the feeling of having a say in daily operations, you are already halfway to a positive change reaction.

Avenues for future research might include a study of the format, or type of communication, used to inform employees initially of change in relation to initial change reaction. The form of communication used to convey the information might influence employees' initial experience with organizational change. For example, initial change communication could take the form of a live, in-person

---

[64] Judge, W., Bowler, M., & Douglas, T. (2006). Preparing for organizational change: Evolution of the organizational capacity for change construct. Academy of Management Annual Meeting Proceedings, 01–06. http://dx.doi.org/10.5465/AMBPP.2006.27169501

meeting, a web-based meeting with video, a teleconference, a memo sent through the mail or email. Since the type of the initial change communication can vary, the type of format used to convey organizational change might influence employees' initial reaction to change. In general, it is a good idea to start with an in-person conversation if possible. Video and web conferences are also good options if in-person conversations are challenging for various reasons, including travel cost.

To improve the probability of a more positive change reaction, all four independent variables must be considered before, during, and after implementing large-scale change, as individually they do not influence reaction to change. Although the association was only directional and not significant, based on the multiple regression analysis, change leaders should pay particular attention to the mode and content of the initial change communication as it could influence whether employees support or resist organizational change.

A well-coordinated process that considers a variety of change dimensions is needed for successful change implementation. Such a process might consist of an approach that does not single out any one predictor, but employs a combination of all four predictors (initial change reaction, involvement in change design, perceived change success, and change communication) that can assist in creating an environment of successful organizational change.

As noted in the sample characteristics, one participant in my study was a change management expert with Six Sigma expertise. A close examination of the responses from this participant revealed that the participant responded very positively to the questions related to the championing subscale of support of change. The participant was actively involved in the change process, perceived the quality and frequency of change-related communication highly favorably, and scored perceived change success very highly. The responses also indicate that the participant maintained an optimistic perspective of the change, and influenced others to support the change. This participant essentially modeled the behaviors implied in my recommended actions to improve the probability of successful organizational change.

We now know that a combination of actions representing the four independent variables (initial change reaction, involvement in change design, perceived change success, and change communication) influences reaction to change. We also know that in the pharmaceutical industry, these variables independently do not influence reaction to change. When focused on the supportive side of employee response to change, ranging from mere compliance to enthusiastic championing, the four independent variables (in aggregate or individually) did not influence support of change. However, the four independent variables significantly predicted the championing subscale of support of change. In addition, the findings of this study support the use of transformational leadership and stakeholder theory, but to a lesser extent the use of Lewin's change management model to inform and frame organizational change.

The following two areas of focus, if executed well, may foster a positive or supportive reaction to change. They address aspects of the four independent variables which my study demonstrated influences reaction to change, and the championing subscale of support of change when considered together as a package.

1) The communication plan ensures the frequency and quality of communication, which can, in turn, elicit a positive initial reaction if handled well.

2) Leveraging a network of change agents to interact with employees at all levels of the organization is a good way to keep employees and upper management involved. Doing so gives employees a voice and a feeling that their opinions and concerns matter, and it gives upper management a handle on progress and a favorable reputation when they listen to suggestions along the way, all of which could give an overall feeling that the change may be successful.

Although the results of my study confirm that change is best examined as a multidimensional construct, the factors of the construct might be particular to the organizational needs and change dynamics of the pharmaceutical industry. As such, the study offers researchers encouragement and direction to identify additional factors—specific to the industry of practice—to help predict employee response to change. It also creates an opportunity to develop a better understanding of the connection between employee support of change, and the enthusiasm employees feel for change as stakeholders in any industry.

Finally, the findings that only a small percent of employees resist change, and a majority of those who support change merely comply provides an opportunity for managers to create enthusiasm and build support for change, starting with the initial change communication. Doing so might convert some of the few that may otherwise resist change or may be ambivalent toward it, and move them up the change reaction spectrum.

Additional Survey Responses

Respondent Experience in Large-Scale Change Initiative

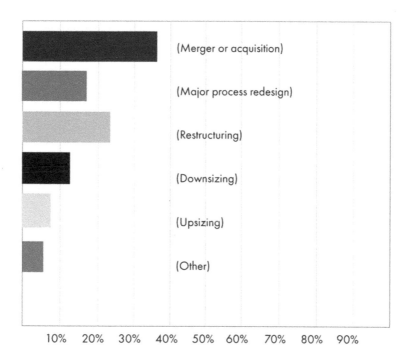

- (Merger or acquisition)
- (Major process redesign)
- (Restructuring)
- (Downsizing)
- (Upsizing)
- (Other)

10% 20% 30% 40% 50% 60% 70% 80% 90%

COMPLIANCE

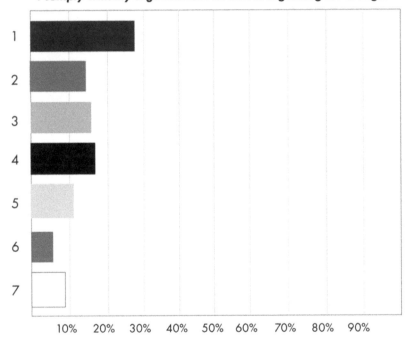

Respondents Answers: 1= strongly disagree   7= strongly agree
'I comply with my organizations directives regarding the change.'

COMPLIANCE

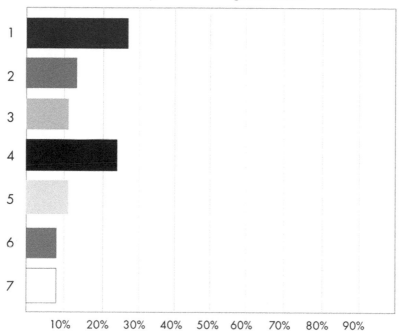

Respondents Answers: 1= strongly disagree   7= strongly agree
'I accept the role changes involved.'

COMPLIANCE

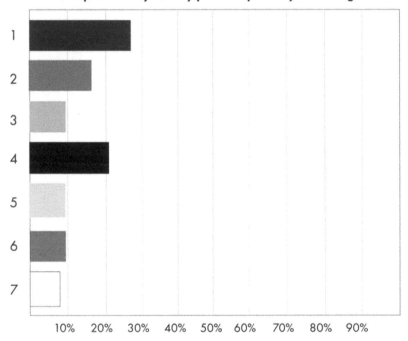

Respondents Answers: 1= strongly disagree   7= strongly agree
'I adjust the way I do my job as required by this change.'

COOPERATION

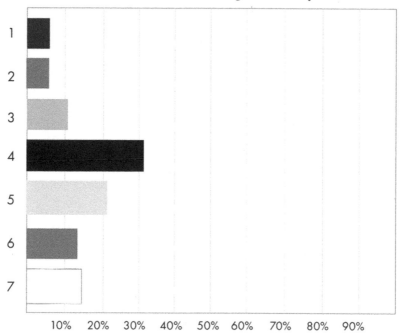

Respondents Answers: 1= strongly disagree   7= strongly agree
'I work toward the change consistently.'

COOPERATION

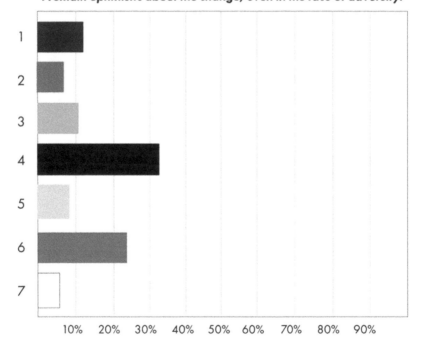

Respondents Answers: 1= strongly disagree   7= strongly agree
'I remain optimistic about the change, even in the face of adversity.'

COOPERATION

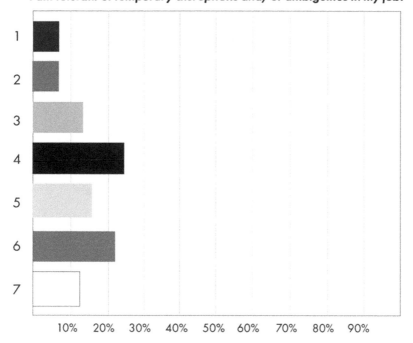

Respondents Answers: 1= strongly disagree   7= strongly agree
'I am tolerant of temporary disruptions and/or ambiguities in my job.'

COOPERATION

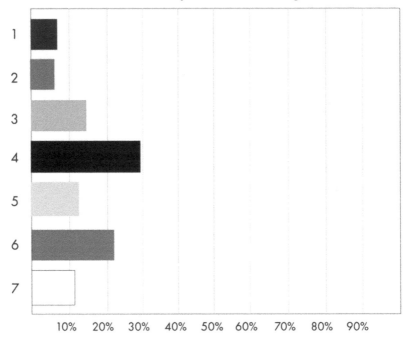

Respondents Answers: 1= strongly disagree   7= strongly agree
'I don't complain about the change.'

COOPERATION

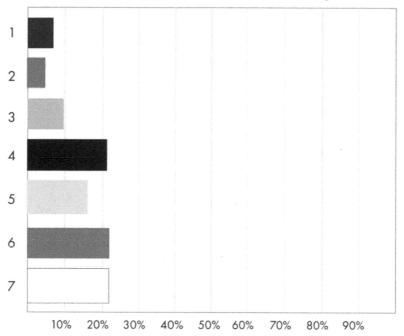

Respondents Answers: 1= strongly disagree   7= strongly agree
'I try to keep myself informed about the change.'

COOPERATION

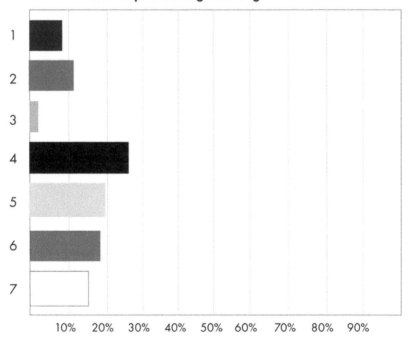

Respondents Answers: 1= strongly disagree   7= strongly agree
'I seek help concerning the change when needed.'

COOPERATION

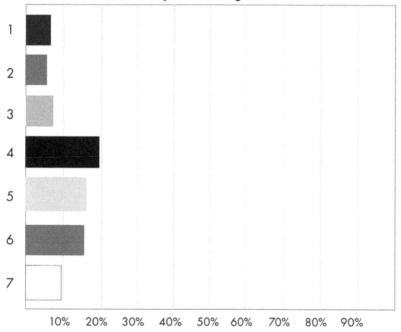

Respondents Answers: 1= strongly disagree   7= strongly agree
'I engage in change related behaviors that seem difficult in the short-term but are likely to have long-term benefits.'

COOPERATION

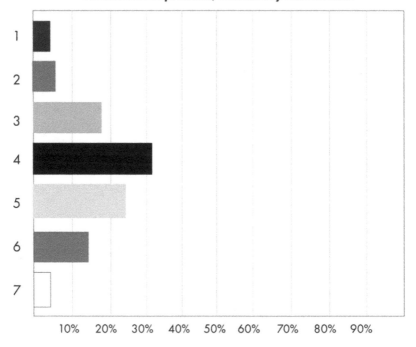

Respondents Answers: 1= strongly disagree   7= strongly agree
'I avoid former practices, even if they seem easier.'

COOPERATION

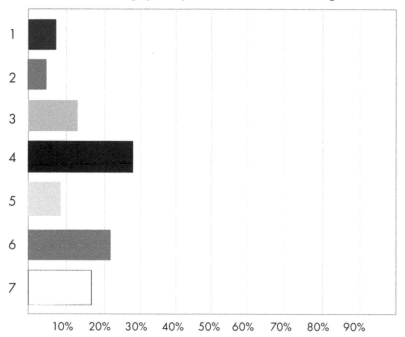

Respondents Answers: 1= strongly disagree   7= strongly agree
'I encourage participation of others in the change.'

CHAMPIONING

Respondents Answers: 1= strongly disagree   7= strongly agree
'I speak positively about the change to co-workers.'

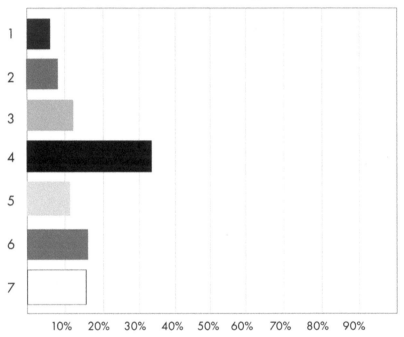

CHAMPIONING

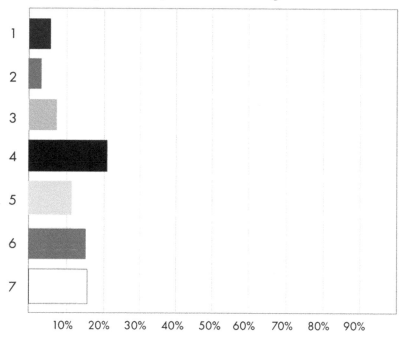

Respondents Answers: 1= strongly disagree   7= strongly agree
'I try to find ways to overcome change difficulties.'

CHAMPIONING

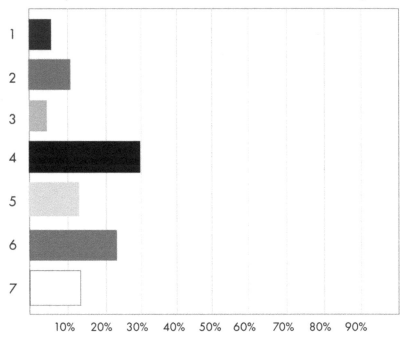

Respondents Answers: 1= strongly disagree   7= strongly agree
'I try to overcome co-workers' resistance toward the change.'

CHAMPIONING

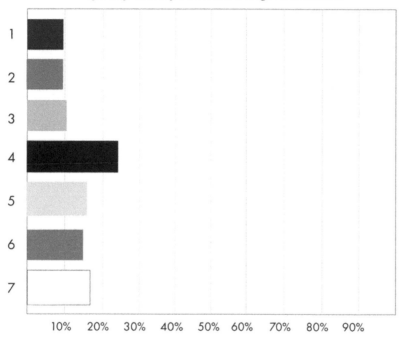

Respondents Answers: 1= strongly disagree   7= strongly agree
'I speak positively about the change to outsiders.'

CHAMPIONING

About the Author

Dr. Otis Johnson started out in the pharmaceutical industry doing basic research in an immunology lab at New York University School of Medicine. He then transitioned to clinical research at Merck, where he spent a total of thirteen years in various scientific and operations roles. Dr. Johnson has a key eye for identifying ways to improve efficiency, and always did value-added work outside of his core job description. One notable value-added project he did as a clinical scientist was writing and producing a professional-grade training video to reduce travel costs associated with worldwide travel to train trial nurses, physicians, and study coordinators how to perform quality lung function tests consistently.

Because of this quality, Dr. Johnson was asked to participate in a major restructuring initiative at Merck to improve the efficiency of its scientific and operational divisions. This project led to the creation of a dedicated patient recruitment and feasibility department intended to facilitate better planning and execution of clinical trials. He later joined this dedicated group and founded a clinical informatics function that provided all the analytics that supported feasibility and patient recruitment for clinical trials.

Dr. Johnson and his team began tracking metrics rigorously and were able to show that when his team was involved in planning and running clinical trials, the trials his team was involved in were more likely to finish on time. These performance metrics were largely responsible for the full team making it through the Merck-Schering Plough merger fully intact while there were large employee reductions in other parts of the company.

Through an industry contact familiar with his presentations and publications, he later joined a CRO to lead a struggling feasibility group. He rapidly transformed the group into a state-of-the-art feasibility and clinical informatics function, a result he won an operational excellence award for and a promotion to vice president.

Dr. Johnson has a Bachelor of Science degree in Health Science with a concentration in Medical Laboratory Sciences, a Master of Public Administration (MPA) in Health Policy & Management from New York University, and a PhD in Management with a specialization in Leadership and Organizational Change.

CPSIA information can be obtained
at www.ICGtesting.com
Printed in the USA
LVHW07s1134030918
588984LV00027B/298/P